The Restaurant-(The L

Anecdote 1

"How many?
"Get the menus."
"Sure, we can seat a party of ten."
People were coming in droves. I couldn't believe what a
gold mine we built in just a short amount of time.
Our restaurant was buzzing.
It was the talk of the town.
He was on the cook line, cooking his heart out.
Mom was in the front hosting.
I was behind the counter answering the phones.
People came from all over just to get a seat at our
new place.
We waited patiently for the restaurant's first review.
It was our first month in business.
The review came out and they were raving.
They commented- *"deft hand in the kitchen."*
He was happy.
I was happy.
Our customers were happy.
It couldn't get any better than this.
Every night was busy.
Every night was packed.
We were so fortunate.
I remember cashing out the register one night. I told him I'd
meet him home.
I put the money into our safe and I waited anxiously for
him to pull up.
I had just gotten my teaching job and we just opened up a
successful business so I know this wasn't the perfect time,
but when is it ever the perfect time?
I heard the car pull up and I greeted him anxiously
at the door.
I had a small present in my hand.
"Here, open it."

He looked at me in astonishment and begins to tear the paper off. He stared at it and at first he didn't get it at all.
'No!"
"No way!"
"I'm going go to be a father." I'm going to be a father!"
In less than five seconds, he grabbed a pot and a pan and began banging them in harmony, running up and down the road.
"What are you crazy? Get in here. You'll wake up the neighbors."
But I couldn't take this moment away. This very special moment.
I could hear him screaming as loud as he could, "I'm going to be a father.
Hey everybody, did you hear me? We're going to have a baby."
Yes, life is going just as planned.

Wake up! (Darkness-2)

Anecdote 2

"Wake up!"
He nudged me.
I got startled. I had just fallen asleep.
I looked at the clock. It's 11:00 p.m The kids are
fast asleep.
"What, what's wrong?"
I followed him as he leads me into the living room.
Christmas decorations filled the room and animated
figurines were strategically placed right in front of the tree.
We had just bought white themed ornaments and beautiful
silver bows to accent the tree.
The decorations looked magical. The kids were so excited
for Christmas this year. They were at the perfect age.
*"Look! Look!" Don't you see them? There! A million ants
are crawling on the ceiling.*
*"What do you mean a million ants are on the ceiling? I
don't see any.*
Just go back to sleep."
*"Look, look they're all over. And look at Mr. and Mrs.Claus,
they're dancing."*
"They're not dancing."
"Just wait. They'll dance.
I waited patiently as he stared right at them. Not even a
blink in sight, so as not to miss them dance.
"See, they just danced."
"What's wrong with you? They are completely still."
I have no idea what's come over him.
*"Call your cousin and ask him why he dropped these elves
over."*
*"I'm not calling there. Are you crazy? It's the middle of
the night."*
For some reason I knew this wasn't going to end anytime
soon so I pretended to call.

"He said he didn't drop any elves over. It's late and he's sleeping."

"But I left money on the mantle and they took it.

"Who took it?"

I looked around in dismay. I'm exhausted. I just want to go to bed.

"Those elves that are hiding behind the couch took it."

I proceeded to the couch and look over to see the elves. No elves in sight. Not a surprise.

He led me to the kitchen.

"And look I left apple pie on the table and they took a bite"

"Who ate it? What the hell are you talking about? Are you sure you didn't eat it? Just go to sleep. It's late. You're going to wake up the kids. You're just having a nightmare."

A nightmare. At this point, it was no longer a nightmare. He was hallucinating.

I lead him back to the couch hoping that he would fall asleep there.

But he began his rants again.

"They're all over. Don't you see them. They're on the walls and the ceilings. They're all over…all over…all over.."

"Shhhh. What the hell has gotten into you?"

My voice then became louder. I could no longer entertain this.

"You need to go to sleep. For the last damn time, go to sleep. I have to go to work in three hours."

And the cycle repeated itself all throughout the late hours of the night and into the early morning.

I never went to bed that night.

But he finally did.

It's going to be a long day.

He's Arrived- (The Light-3)

Anecdote 3

*"You promised me the epidural. You promised at 4
centimeters you would give me the f***'n epidural."*
Time froze. It felt like a lifetime. I have never felt pain
like this.
The pain intensified within seconds from being induced.
I held on to the sides of the bed. I thought my stomach
would explode.
Finally, I reached ten centimeters.
He was with me. Pacing back and forth.
I began to push. I pushed. I pushed with all my might but I
felt nothing .
The epidural had finally kicked in. Our baby didn't want to
make an appearance. It's already two weeks late.
He came to my side every second of the minute. I couldn't
hold down the ice chips.
I vomited. I vomited again at every push. I just couldn't
push anymore. I just couldn't.
It's been 14 hours.
I was exhausted.
The doctor looked worried. He sends me in for a
sonogram.
I heard them whispering that our baby was in distress.
"What does that mean? What does that even mean?"
I began to shake.
*"We have to do an emergency c-section. The baby's
umbilical cord may be wrapped around it's neck causing it
to be distressed."*
I looked at him and he looked at me and I began to cry.
5-4-3-2-1 I'm in surgery, just like that.
I felt a tug.
I felt a pull.
I felt more tugs and more pulls and more tugs and more
pulls.

I hear a loud cry. It's the most beautiful sound I have ever heard.

"It's a boy."

My heart melted.

"A beautiful, healthy baby boy."

Luca is finally here.

Our family awaits the good news. Champagne pops in the waiting room. Everyone is drinking champagne.

He is the happiest he has ever been.

He holds Luca for the first time and begins to call him by his nickname, "Mini me." And that he sure was.

His mini me.

This was one of the best days of my life.

Life just can't get better than this.

It just can't.

No Answer (Darkness-4)

Anecdote 4

The kids were bathed and almost ready for bed. I always loved bath time with the kids and so did they.
But it was getting late. He usually got home on time.
I called his phone. No answer. I called again and again. I became relentless with calling.
Nothing. No answer once again. The waiting was killing me.
"Where the hell is he?"
I leave another message. And another. And another.
It's 8:30 p.m
The phone rang.
 "Hi, is this Mrs. Marra?"
The phone call everyone is always afraid to get. That dreadful call. I can't believe I had gotten that call.
"Yes."
"Your husband was in an accident and you need to get to the hospital.
My heart sank.
"What? How? When?"
"You can get more details when you get there."
Why can't they just tell you if they're o.k?
I worry about the kids. I always worry about the kids. I gave them a kiss and dropped them off to family.
I called my boss from the car. He hears it in my voice.
"What's wrong?"
"I'm on the way to the hospital. I don't know when I'll be in this week. Just get me coverage. He's been in an accident and that's all I know so far. I don't think it's good."
Every possible scenario raced through my mind. Did he break his back? Is he recognizable? Is he in surgery?Is he even alive? What will I tell the kids?"
I had absolutely no idea.
The officer did not elaborate. I had no idea what was in store for me once I got there.

So I embraced for the worst.

I raced to get there, zig zagging in between traffic. Nobody was going fast enough.

Nobody ever goes fast enough when you're in a rush.

I pulled up and parked behind an ambulance. The hospital was so busy that night.

I spot him but someone was holding him up right by the hospital entrance. They walked towards me.

"What the hell is going on?"

"The car is totaled, but he's fine. Just get him home. He doesn't want to go in."

"What do you mean he's fine?"

He is definitely not fine.

They could see the disappointment and worry on my face. I stutter.

"But, but he was just at work."

My stomach was in knots. I needed answers. I needed them now.

I'm raging inside. Raging.

He could barely get a word out in the car ride home. He stuttered. He mumbled.

Who is this man? And what happened?

I get him home.

He passes out.

No story.

No reasons.

And no answers.

A Sign (The Light-5)

Anecdote 5

"*Max if it's a boy. Ava Lo'ren if it's a girl.*"
We knew no matter what the sonogram showed us that we had our baby names all
picked out.
We didn't find out what the gender of our first child was, but there we were, not even seven months after Luca was born, waiting patiently to find out the gender of our second child.
I was so nervous. They would only be 13 months apart.
Anxiety set in, but I was still elated to add to our family.
But how could I manage to take care of them all by myself?
He would work all day and through the night and I had to work full time. I knew it wasn't going to be easy, but our life was going so well. We were so fortunate to have all this. Why stop now?
I couldn't help but feel blessed to have another child.
There we were in the waiting room anxiously waiting for the big five month sonogram. Oh how we loved that five month sonogram.
We knew the names of Baby X, but now we needed to confirm what gender it was.
As we waited, I grabbed the closest fashion magazine and started flipping through the pages. I flipped the first page.
"*Hmmm.*" And then another and then another.
"*Well, that's strange.*"
I couldn't believe it. I couldn't believe that this particular magazine issue just confirmed the sex of our baby. It was a sign. A sure sign.
"*Look!*" I flipped the page.
"*And look!*" I flipped another and another.
"*It's a boy...It's going to be a boy. Holy sh*t another boy.* Luca's going to be so happy."
"*How do you know?*"

Each page displayed elaborate fashion collections by the well known designer, Max Mara.

Atop each page, and there were several of them, read **Max Mara** in bold letters.

I knew right then and there it was going to be a boy.

Our time came. We entered the room and the technician began to prep my belly.

The sonogram looked normal. We were so happy.

And indeed it was confirmed. We were having a baby boy. He was so happy that another boy will soon carry his name and I was thrilled Luca would have a baby brother to play with.

In four months, Max Marra would soon enter the world. I just couldn't wait to meet him.

Life just seems to get better and better.
Nothing could ruin this moment.
Absolutely nothing.

Naïve (Darkness-6)

Anecdote 6

"What the hell are these?"
No reply.
"One more time, what in the hell are these? I know you hear me."
I yelled it across the house to make sure he heard.
"What? Why are you yelling?"
"Not really yelling- just wondering what these were and why they were in this house.
Waiting for an answer."
I held up the ziploc bag.
"They're nothing. Don't be dumb. Just give them to me."
He most definitely could have taken them from me, but he didn't. At this point, I held the bag of pills up high.. Approximately 15 monstrous white pills. I hadn't a clue what they were. They seemed impossible to swallow. I couldn't believe they had made pills this size.
"I swear to you, I better not find out that you're actually taking these, whatever the hell they are, pills."
"They're just pills. They're just like Advil."
"I have not once ever heard you complain about any pain. I guess you won't be needing them then."
"Stop, just give them to me."
He chuckled. He actually chuckled. He wasn't worried in the least.
"It's not funny. And I'm not giving them to you."
He finally goes for the ziploc bag, as if I would have given up so easily, but I wouldn't have it. I refused to let them go.
"Seriously Claudia, they're harmless. Take one and you'll see."
"I'm not taking one of these damn pills….and guess what, neither will you. There is absolutely no reason why you need these frig'n ridiculous looking horse pills."
I may have been a bit naïve, but I have never taken a pill that looked like these before. If he says they were like Advil

then I will take his word for it for now, but my gut feeling is saying different. One thing I knew was I was sure as sh*t not giving them back.

"Don't you ....don't you dare. You're making a big deal out of nothing."

I headed out the door, ziploc in hand. I began to drive off. He followed me in his car.

Before I even got off our road, I rolled down my window, waved the bag so he could see exactly what I was about to do. I opened the bag of horse pills and dumped every single one of them outside my car window. I was clearly being a bitch.

They hit the pavement in unison. Just like that.

He was definitely pissed.

And honestly, in hindsight, I had no idea what I had just done,

but it just felt so good to do it.

I hadn't looked for or found a ziploc bag since.

Or maybe he just got better at hiding them.

Home Sweet Home – (The Light-7)

Anecdote 7

He grabbed the bags and the car seat and placed them in the car.

We were ready. I grabbed Luca from my mother's arms.

"Give mommy a big kiss. I'm going to miss you so much."

I gave Luca a big kiss and hug as we got ready for a scheduled C- section.

I was advised to schedule a C-section because it was dangerous to give birth naturally so soon after your first c-section. So that is what I did.

We needed to be at the hospital by 11:30 a.m. All was going as planned.

We were ready and excited for the arrival of our second baby boy.We arrived right on time. The doctors prepped me and prepped him. He was allowed to be in the room during the birth. He wanted to be the first to meet his new son.

It's amazing how I could talk to the doctor during my surgery. I felt nothing from the neck down except for those tugs and pulls. It felt so weird and incredible at the same time.

At 2:30, Max Marra entered the world.

I held him for a split second. He was so adorable. He held him for a few seconds more and then they whisked me off to the recovery room.

Oh how I forgot about the recovery. It was god awful. I was nauseous. I was so nauseous. I was freezing. It was always freezing in the recovery room.

I was completely out of it. I had no energy left. My eyes kept rolling into the back of my head at the start of every nauseous moment. I just wanted to vomit, but I couldn't.

He came to visit me to see how I was doing. I was shivering. I could only move my head.

I looked at him. He didn't seem like himself.

"Something's wrong. They took Max to N.I.C.U. They said he will be okay, but...."
I took it in. I took it all in.
"Please, please just get out. I can't even. I can't even think right now."
My head was about to explode. I couldn't feel my body yet. I had to recover. I just needed a few more minutes. He respected that. I am sure he was just as afraid as I was. Panic set in. I was an emotional mess.
What was he saying? I saw him. I held him. He was beautiful and healthy. I was just so sick that I didn't even have the energy to think. And then right there, I could see my aunt's eyes through the tiny glass of the recovery room. She was watching me.
Those eyes. They could speak to you. I will never forget her stare. It was full of worry.
I could tell in an instant just from her eyes that my baby was not okay.
I called for my doctor. He knew I was worried.
"Everything is going to be okay. Max swallowed some meconium during the surgery and he had some issues breathing. He was only taken to N.I.C.U as a precaution, but he is 100 percent fine now. I waited until they were sure so I could come tell you the good news."
"Is he okay though, please tell me he will be okay."
"He is fine. They're only observing him. It's very normal for babies to swallow meconium during a C-section birth. I promise you, he's fine, he's healthy and breathing perfectly fine on his own."
I was so relieved. I couldn't wait to hold my baby boy. N.I.C.U at the time was in another wing. Being that it was not on my floor, I couldn't visit Max yet. I was so stressed out. My doctor had not given me the okay. I still had to recover.
Daddy took over for me. He changed Max and fed him for two days until I was strong enough to take over. He did a great job. They truly bonded.
Luca would have been a little jealous. He truly loved

his little boys.

Two days passed and I finally got to visit my beautiful baby. He was so chubby. He was so cute. We called him "Little Buddha."

He was healthy and that was all that mattered to me.

After five days of observation, we finally took Max home to meet his brother.

Maybe life didn't always go as planned.

We had a little scare but right at this moment our life was perfect.

We had two beautiful, healthy sons.

Our family was complete.

Ah, home sweet home.

Surprise! (The Light-8)
Anecdote 8

The money was coming in. We had more than we had ever imagined.

Our restaurant was thriving. It was in fact one of our town's most popular places to eat.

With popularity, came customers, many customers, with customers, came cash money.

A lot of cash money. We had it. I'm not going to lie. We went on lavish vacations, remodeled our home from top to bottom, built the boys a beautiful pool and bought fancy cars. We even hired a live in nanny to help with the kids. If things stayed like this, we would have been set for life.

He'd been working so hard. Night after night. He hadn't taken a day off in weeks.

One night he had come home early.

"Close your eyes."

He led me to the driveway.

"What is it?"

I couldn't wait. I slightly cheated. I couldn't believe my eyes. A brand new convertible Mercedes SL 500 was sitting right in our driveway.

This car stood out.

It was sleek, shiny, black, and bold. It was beautiful. It looked like a black panther ready to pounce. I don't know why it was sitting in our driveway. I had the Mercedes truck already and he had a smaller Mercedes Sedan. We did not need another car, especially this kind of car.

"Do you like it?"

I wasn't sure how I felt. I wanted to yell at him for not telling me at first. But I couldn't deny it. I loved it.

He threw me the keys.

"Go ahead, drive it."

I couldn't believe this was ours. And I wasn't really talking about the car. I was talking about this life.

He was only 25. I was just a few years older. He was so young but had the world at his feet.

He was going to make something of himself. He was going to build a legacy for his children.

And it was that night, that very night, that you could see it in his eyes that nothing would get between him and his family. He worked too hard. He was reaching for the top.

He would have done anything for his boys. He adored them. He absolutely adored them.

I started the car and rode off into the night.

The world was mine.

At least for tonight it was.

If Only Fish Could Talk (Darkness-9)
Anecdote 9

I walked in from work. I went straight for my boys. They were still so little.
I hated leaving them.I hugged and kissed them. I just wanted to breathe them in.
"Mommy missed you today. How were they today? How'd they eat? Did they have their milk?"
My nanny didn't answer. She eyeballed me to look over into the den.
I was confused. I headed for the den and there he was, somewhat out of it.
"What are you doing home?"
I was even more confused. He rarely left the restaurant.
My cousin Joey was with him on the couch. No answer from either of them.
"Joos like dat-he fall down and your cousin he take him to the hospital. I don't know. I don't know what got into mister. Ask him."
My nanny was from Guyana. I remember her adorable accent. She was the absolute best. She always watched out for us. I trusted her with my life. But this shook her. It really shook her. I wished I could have asked her more questions.
He lifted his head and just blurted out that he was fine. I looked at my cousin in disbelief. He didn't really know what to say to me.
"We just got home from lunch. He was staring into the fish tank and he just collapsed. Just like that. He just nearly missed Max."
He had bought a 100 gallon fish tank just days before. He filled the tank with these beautiful, exotic fish. At this stage of the game, he no longer was simple.
He had to have the extreme. He had to have the best.

He knew the boys would have loved them and that they did. They loved it.

"What? He almost missed Max. How could that be?"

I grabbed Max. Luckily, he was just fine.

"Bibi and I tried to get him up. He sat for a half and hour. I finally convinced him to go the hospital."

"So what did the doctor say?"

"He's fine. Completely fine. Before we walked out of there he bought everyone pizza."

"Are you serious?"

I went over to him. He seemed more awake now.

"Are you okay? What happened?'

"I'm fine. I just got a little dizzy and fainted."

"Well, that's not normal. What did the doctor say? "

"He said I was probably dehydrated and run down. I'm fine."

"So you'll stay home then. You better stay home. People just don't collapse out of the blue."

"Yeah, Yeah, Yeah."

"I'm serious."

And not even five minutes later, he was out the door again.

And there I was trying to put the pieces together of what actually transpired

here today.

It was a day of strange answers

and strange behavior.

I picked Max up again and headed to the fish tank.

If only fish could talk.

Angelo- 10 (The Light and Darkness)
Anecdote 10

"Nope, we are not getting a dog. Hell no, no, no."
"Oh come on, The boys will love it. Especially Luca."
"No way. Do you understand that Luca just got out of diapers and Max is still in diapers? You also realize that I work, right, and will not be home."
"Oh stop. Come on. Can you imagine the kid's faces when they see it?"
"Who is going to walk it and pick up after it? Nope, not me, not now. Not until they get older. And where will you be? Oh of course not home. You'll be at work all day and night."
"Oh stop, it won't be that bad."
"I refuse to take care of another baby. I absolutely refuse. So don't even think about it."

This was the way this conversation went for about six months. And don't get me wrong, I am an animal lover but I knew exactly how this would pan out. I'd be stuck picking up crap, walking it and feeding it in addition to cleaning up after the boys.

And not to mention Bibi was deathly afraid of dogs, all kinds of dogs. And just because of this known fact that our nanny was deathly afraid, I thought it was safe to say that we will not be owning a dog for a very long time to come.

I had gone to work and from work I went to a meeting. I remember pulling up to the house around 4:30. I was exhausted. I just wanted to change and relax.

As I entered the house, I could see the kitchen from the doorway. I couldn't believe it.

I just couldn't believe it. I scanned the entire counter. I took a double take to make sure that what I saw was actually real.

What I didn't see though were the kids, Bibi, nor did I see him.

"What in the world is all this?"

You could hear me from the other room.

At this point, I'm fuming.

He comes waltzing into the kitchen, smiling of course. I looked at him and I pointed at the counter.

"You are kidding me, right?"

On the counter was everything you could possibly imagine that was needed to take care of a new puppy. I saw training pads, I saw wipes, I saw a crate, I saw food, I saw bones, I saw chewy toys. I saw it all. Our kitchen was a full blown pet store.

And not even a few seconds later, I see an adorable English Bull Dog puppy waddling through the hall coming right for me. My jaw dropped. It plopped itself right at my feet. And of course right on its tail was Luca.

"Mommy, mommy, this is Angelo."

He said it in the sweetest voice. I think he already fell in love.

"ANGELO? You named him already?"

I couldn't believe the exact thing that I did not need in my life right now was sitting at the bottom of my feet and to boot it already had a name, Angelo.

I looked at him. He was still smiling from his outrageous purchase.

"Just look at his face. It's the cutest face ever. You can't deny that face."

I didn't say a word. I didn't look at Angelo. I didn't look at him.

His heart was in the right place, but he did not fully think this through.

I walked out of the kitchen to change. I took a deep breathe and headed back into the den. There was no way we were keeping this puppy even as cute as it was.

Luca was content playing with Angelo. Max was just too little to understand and

Dad was sitting on the couch watching television.

I decided to sit my tired ass on the couch just opposite him. There was no way in hell I was lifting a finger to take care of this puppy. He wanted it, so now he is going to take care of it. My plate was full. I was done. It was cute though. It was really cute, but I couldn't admit it. I did not budge. I had to be a bitch. I just had to. This was a big deal.

Within an hour, the whole house smelled. He got a headache. I got a headache.

"Are you happy now? Are you happy that you bought a puppy that you now have to take care of, oh wait that I have to take care of? And now look at your son, he is already attached to it."

Nothing was a big deal to him. But I stuck to my word that I was not helping. I grabbed Luca and Max. It was time for them to get ready for bed. Luca gave Angelo a big hug. It was very sweet and I got ready for bed too. As I started to doze off, I could hear the sounds of Angelo whimpering through my bedroom wall hour after hour after hour.

It killed me.
I finally pulled the blanket over my head,
put the volume on the television just a tad bit
louder
and passed out.
I had a great night sleep that night.
At least one of us did.

Sold (Darkness-11)
Anecdote 11

It truly was his baby, but after much contemplation
and negotiation, they shook hands.
The restaurant was now under new ownership.
We were lucky to sell our restaurant while it was flourish-
ing. He had been thinking about it for some time.
He wanted to franchise. He was a good business man with
great ideas.
We had made a pretty penny off of the sale.
And even though we didn't have to worry for years to
come, he went right out there to try and find the perfect
location to recreate his restaurant.
And he did just that. He opened two more.
But this time was different.
He didn't put the time into them like he did with his first
one.
His love and passion for cooking started to diminish. He
began leaving the restaurant
and coming home more during the day.
He began taking off nights and spending a lot of time at
home. He was afraid to leave the kids for some reason. He
had missed them and they missed him. It started to become a habit. He would watch the news day in and day
out. The boys would actually walk around the den and
chant, *"No more news. No more news."*
He would be home almost everyday when I got there. It
was so unlike him. At times,
I'd find him napping while the nanny took care of the boys.
His workers would call him and he wouldn't answer his
phone. They would stop by and I would have to tell them
he wasn't home. I became worried. I tried to talk to him.
Nothing got through to him.
"I'm fine." That's all he would say.

One day I caught him in the driveway. We both pulled in at the same time.

"Where were you?"

"I went to my doctor."

"Doctor? For what? Which doctor?"

"I hurt my toe. Think I broke it."

"When? Let me see. Doctors can't do anything for a broken toe."

"Yeah I know but I found this awesome guy. I've seen him a few times before. His office is by my old house."

"By your old house? That's too far. Are you nuts? Why would you go all that way?"

"You'd love him. You have to go see him. At least once. I'm telling you, he's a good guy. He told me just to tape them together."

His strange behavior continued after this. He even started walking with a cane. A cane. I couldn't even fathom why. It was a broken toe for f***s sake. It was just so odd. Several days passed. He didn't show up at the restaurant at all. The days turned into several weeks.

He'd have his workers close up.

He would sleep.

He would go out.

He would sleep.

Then go out. Same routine, everyday. Where the hell was he going?

His toe had gotten better and the cane disappeared.

We began to fight. We began to fight a lot, but never in front of the kids.

I couldn't put up with his shit anymore. His behavior became unpredictable.

I was a loving wife. He had two beautiful young sons at home. He adored us.

Something happened.

Something happened that changed our perfect world forever.

The Searching (Darkness-12)
Anecdote 12

There he laid. His motionless body passed out on the bed.
It's only 3:30 in the afternoon.
He didn't even know we walked in.
I placed the kid's backpacks in the hall and I set them up in
front of the t.v.
Where did he put it?
I ransacked the house. I looked in the cabinets, I looked
under the bed, even under the mattress, I looked in the
empty boxes of cereal and even the full boxes. I knew they
were here. I can smell them. Each and every one of them.
All the places I knew he had hidden them before.
I stared into our bedroom as he laid there numb and I saw
the night stand. I crawled under and I felt my way around. I
reached as far as I could and there it was right in the palm
of my hand.
The big orange bottle of god damn pills. I found the mother
load. He taped it to the bottom
of the nightstand. How clever. I ripped the tape off and
pulled it from underneath the nightstand. I rushed to the
bathroom and flushed them down the toilet as quickly
as I could.
I headed back to the room to tape the empty pill bottle
back under the nightstand. Empty…
I quietly headed out of the room but I'd become smarter.
I've learned to crawl just so I wouldn't wake him. I stood up
as I got into the hallway. I was safe. I could breathe again.
This became routine. It was so hard to talk sense into
someone that had an addiction.
So I smartened up and just started dumping them.
All of them.
"What the hell are you doing?"
My skin crawled.
"Claudia!"

I panicked. He had gotten up out of his stupor.

Shit, the kids will hear him.

I made it to the kitchen and pretended to take the pots out to cook. My heart raced.

My thoughts were in a whirlwind. I wanted to scream. I wanted to punch him in the face.

I wanted to— I don't know what I wanted to do, but I know I can no longer do this thing called life with him.

I could hear his breathing through the walls.

His disheveled hair, his wife beater tank and his depleted look. His youthful face seemed to be a distant memory.

"Where did you put it?" Stop playing around. Where did you put it?"

"I have no idea. Don't ask me. Maybe you took them all and don't remember. And lower your god damn voice so the kids won't hear you."

He began to search. The searching. The endless searching. I just couldn't take the searching anymore.

For every pillow he flipped, for every draw he rummaged through, for every cereal box he emptied, my heart would beat a million beats a minute.

He staggered through the hall and passed out on the bed once again.

I took a long, deep breath.

Inhale. Exhale.

I held my kids close.

Unsuccessful searches this time, but I call it a win.

The Move (Darkness – 13)

Anecdote 13

We had sold our home and purchased another close to his old neighborhood.

Days came and went.

He did nothing but stay home. No job in sight except occasional small jobs that he did with his family.

He was able to put the boys on the bus and get them in the afternoon.

The new bus stop was only a few houses away. They loved that daddy would be there for them. They looked forward to it.

We wanted the kids to have a chance to spend time with his family now.

They lived very close by. It was time that his mom helped watched the boys and it was time to give my mom a break.

He wanted us to have a fresh start. So much had happened. So much.

I wasn't okay with the move. I really wasn't. I fought it. It was hard for me to trust him. But I wanted to keep our family together even if it meant leaving our beautiful home and my family. The kids were just about to start Pre- K and Kindergarten so if we were to do it, now had been the time. The school district was top-notch so I couldn't use that as an excuse. And the boys would get to go to school with their cousins. That was a huge plus.

I was very well aware of his addiction at this stage of the game. Very well aware. I figured moving closer to his family would be good for him.

I had to make the ultimate sacrifice and I had to give this a chance.

It was about the kids. Isn't it always about the kids?

The new house was sort of cute, but I did not love it. I just couldn't get myself to love it.

Actually, I could barely get myself to like it. The neighborhood wasn't very warm and the neighbors kept to themselves. They barely greeted us. I wasn't used to that.

And something about this house was so cold. Something about this house was so eery.

But it was our new home. Our new start. I had to figure it out. At this point, I really had no choice. I was determined to keep our family together.

I sat him down once we settled in.

"This is it. I moved for you. I left my family and our beautiful home so that you can be close with your family again and so that you can get your shit together."

"This is going to be good for me. This is going to be good for us. I'll go to work with my family. I'll be able to get the kids on and off the bus. They'll be so happy."

"I hate it here, but for the sake of our kids I will do my best to make this a beautiful home for them."

And that I did. I did my best to accept our new home.

The kids made new friends. They got to see their cousins a lot. They settled into school with no problems.

They were happy.

He even began to work occasionally. Life was finally moving forward.

Oh wait one last thing,
did I fail to mention
that his doctor,
that hell of a guy that he loved so much
was right in our neighborhood too?
How wonderful.
Oh how freakin' wonderful.

Chinese Food (Darkness-14)

Anecdote 14

I text him. I text him again. No reply.
This seemed to be the norm lately.
Where the hell are you? Answer me!
Nothing.
Twenty minutes went by.
I text again.
Seriously, where the hell are you? Your wife and two kids are home and you're out galavanting. You need to get your ass home.
No reply.
The front door opens at around 11:30.
I stood there with my arms folded.
"What the hell is wrong with you? Where have you been? I have been texting you and texting you."
"I was playing cards."
I could tell he was on something. There were certain times that it was so clear that he was on something and there were other times that he hid it so well.
"Since when do you play cards?"
He dropped the keys on the floor. He hadn't even noticed that they missed the table.
He could barely get himself to the kitchen.
I followed him.
"What's wrong with you? You can barely stand up?"
He was talking, but nothing was making sense.
I had no energy to fight with him and by the looks of it, I was not going to get far any way.
He knocked into the frig and then propped himself up again. But it took him awhile to stand straight.
He went right for the Chinese food, but his movements were in slow motion for some reason. I hated seeing him this bad. We have had endless conversations

and arguments about his addiction. And during every argument, he would promise to get clean. He would promise to stop. I'd yell. I'd cry. I'd beg. Nothing worked. His promises were empty. Absolutely empty.

He scooped out the rice and completely missed the plate. The counter was now full of rice. He attempted to scoop out the chicken and only half of it made it onto the plate this time.

"Seriously, are you okay? This isn't funny. What's gotten into you? You need to just go to sleep." I was scared. I had no idea what I was dealing with. What did he take?

He began sleeping on the couch months ago. He felt safer that way. Don't ask. I hated it because then I couldn't keep an eye on him. I would cringe when I would hear him creeping around the house in the middle of the night. I would never be able to fully close my eyes.

He proceeded to shovel the food onto his fork and it slowly made its way up to his mouth.

The fork steered way to the left and he completely missed his mouth. He then tried it again.

He shoveled more food onto his fork, trying to place it into his mouth and completely misses again. The fork steered all the way to the left once again, no where near his mouth. The food fell all over the floor. There I am cleaning the floors at midnight.

I looked up at him and he was on the counter fast asleep, right on the plate of food.

I couldn't believe it. None of this even phased him. And I knew if I told him, he wouldn't believe it either. He never believed me. He thought I was dramatic.

I took my phone out and started to record him. I recorded every movement and every sound he made, none of which made sense. I was so sick of this shit.

This was the only way that he'd believe me. This was the only way that he could see that he has hit rock bottom and needed to get help. I thought that having two beautiful sons and a loving wife would be enough incentive for him to get help,

but sadly addicts only have one goal and we weren't a part of it.
He climbed onto the couch, leaving a disaster behind him. He passed out temporarily.
I knew he'd be back up again shortly and there was no way I could have fallen asleep knowing he'd be at it again.
So I laid there in my bed
I laid there with my eyes wide open
thinking of a game plan
thinking of a way to pick up the broken pieces
to this f***ed up life
that I did not sign up for.

The Attic (Darkness-15)

Anecdote 15

"Get out! If this is the life you want to lead. Get out. We can't be a part of this anymore."
He tried to blame me for many of our problems, but the bottomline was he had chosen drugs over his family.
We separated for a while. I fought for us for too long. You just can't fight with an addict. They become so selfish and oblivious. I couldn't take what he had become. I think he hated what he had become too. I tried to support him.
I really did. There was just too much water
under the bridge.
The kids didn't know we separated. We told them daddy had to live closer to work, so he can't come home as often anymore. Thankfully, they were too young to understand or question us. Even though his family would help him watch our kids, the fact was I hated leaving the kids, let alone leaving them with him, without me being there.
And there was no way I would let them sleep over there without me. So I started to sleep over there too, which made absolutely no sense.
But It killed me. I worried about them so much. I knew he would never hurt them.
He loved them so much. As addicted as he was, he always showed them so much love.
They didn't know the difference yet, but I could not help but want to protect them.
He was still an addict.
I wanted this to work for the sake of the kids. I really did. I would have sacrificed being unhappy for years to come just so my kids were happy.
I ended up taking him back after three months. He was to come back with he intentions of getting clean. I knew I was being naive.

A week had gone by. Things seemed okay I guess. I just couldn't tell if he was high or not anymore.

He swore he was trying. He swore he hadn't taken anything in a week.

The only times I could really tell if he wasn't high was when he'd run out of pills and go into a withdrawal. I didn't catch on to the withdrawals until years later. He would become deathly ill. He would sweat, get feverish, shake and lay in bed for days. It was just like having the flu. Nothing different. He would say he was sick. He would even go to doctor.

Withdrawals were god awful. At first, I used to tend to him, but after I caught on I would just close the door and leave him be. He had to sweat it out. I wanted no part of them. Withdrawals meant no work for him. No work meant no extra money to pay the bills. Withdrawals also meant he went through his scripts too soon. Technically, he had to wait to see the doctor until he knew his scripts would go through insurance again. I am sure this was a daily struggle for him. I am sure he could think of nothing else but when will he get his pills again.

The week seemed too good to be true. I hadn't witnessed a withdrawal.

I was waiting. Something just wasn't right. I searched all his favorite hiding spots.

I came up with nothing. I was so proud that he made it through the week.

I wanted to believe he was trying. I was happy for my kids the most.

One night I was on the computer upstairs. He was downstairs playing with the kids.

The upstairs wasn't fully finished yet. It was sort of like a storage area for us.

As I was on the computer, I noticed that one of the panels on the wall was slightly ajar. I went over to close it, but got curious so I decided to open it instead. We had just moved in not too long ago so I wasn't familiar with the nooks of the house yet.

I peeked my head in and I didn't see anything. It was clean and empty. I turned to my left and there they were all lined up. Holy shit! It was like a drug store in our attic. I saw an array of bottles. There were about four to five bottles of all different shapes and colors.

This was it. I had it. I called him upstairs. I had them all cradled in my hands and arms.

"Tell me what the hell these are?" It was a rhetorical question. There was no need for an answer.

He didn't know what to say.

"Here I thought you were trying to get clean and you have a stash of this bullshit in our attic."

"I haven't even touched them, I swear."

I didn't believe him.

"This is it. You're a god damn liar."

I was shaking.

"I'm telling you, those have been there."

"Bullshit!"

I had been researching outpatient house rehab while we were separated. I found a doctor that was a few towns over. I had already called.

"I found a doctor that will help you detox. It's an outpatient rehab. He is only a few towns over. If you do not do this for me, if you do not do this for the kids, we are out of here."

"Oh stop. You're not leaving. You're full of crap." His voice was full of confidence.

"I'm telling you, you have to do this, you will do this. You've hit rock bottom and you can't even see it. If you do not go, I am done with you, done with us. I'm making an appointment tomorrow. You're going to rehab."

He agreed. I threw all of his pills out. All of them.

I felt cheated. I felt betrayed.
I felt like I was going to be sick.
I dialed the number and made the appointment.
And all he had to do was show up.

Rehab (The Light-16)
Anecdote 16

"It will be fine. You can do this."

"I know it will. I'll feel better, I know it."

"This will be a new start. You'll get clean. You'll find a good job. You'll see that everything will fall back into place."

I took off from work to go with him to his first appointment at an outpatient rehab. This treatment program will not allow an addict to enroll in the program unless a family member signed the contract with them.

He filled out the paperwork and we waited for the doctor. The first appointment was to last about three hours. I would have waited longer if I had to. This was so important to me. This was so important to our family.

"Hi, I'm Dr. S. What brings you here today?"

I didn't speak. It wasn't my place. This was all him.

"I want to get clean. I'm addicted to painkillers."

"Well, I'm happy you came then. Is there a reason why you were prescribed painkillers?"

"Sometimes my knee hurts."

I have been with him for over five years now and he never complained about his knee.

"How long have you been using?"

"Quite a while."

"How many pills would you say you take a day?'

"Maybe 30-35."

I think he was lying. I would say more.

"Where do you get all these pills?"

"My doctor."

"Okay, Good. I want you to know that you have to be honest with me. Also know that I will notify your doctor that you are enrolled in this program. He will be a part of this treatment as well. We need to cut off your supply. He can no longer write you scripts or you will be kicked out of the program."

I am sure he was devastated about this news. His doctor was his life. His doctor was his priority. I loathed this man. He helped him get addicted. He fed his addiction and made it so easy for him to get his pills.

Whatever he wanted, this doctor gave him. Xanax, Lithium, Methadone, Hydrocodone.

I hadn't a clue. Not one clue that he took so many different pills. In all essence, his doctor was his drug dealer. I couldn't have been happier that his man will no longer be a part of his life.

"I must go over certain rules of the program that you must abide by. If you do not abide by them, you will be kicked out."

"Okay."

I was sure he was sick to his stomach. This was huge.

"You must not take any more painkillers. You must be clean at every appointment. You will take a urine and blood test at every visit. You must take the medicine I prescribe to you as directed. And you must never share your medicine. Do you understand the rules?"

"Yes."

"You will get one warning only. If the tests show any trace of hydrocodone after the warning, then you will be taken out of the program. We will notify your wife and we will not take you back."

We both signed the contract.

The doctor gives him his first dose of Suboxone.

"Suboxone is meant to be used as a component of a drug abuse treatment although you need to know that it still has the potential to be abused. So you will be closely monitored. You will also not receive any more pills than what was prescribed to you. Your wife will hold on to the pills and will give you them as directed. "

"Okay."

"Did you hear him? I have to hold on to them."

We had to wait in the office for two hours while he monitored him on the Suboxone.

The doctor placed the first dose under his tongue.

"The Suboxone has to be placed right under the tongue to dissolve and do not spit it
up at all. If you swallow it then it will not be as effective and it could actually make you vomit."
He nodded.
We waited. I couldn't help to think that I am actually sitting in a rehab treatment center with the man I married, with the father of my two beautiful sons. What has my life come to? What could come of this program? I tried to be his cheerleader. I tried to give him support. I wanted him to know that I will help him through this. I was so happy that today might be the reason that our family stayed together.
Days went by and he was taking the medicine as prescribed. He started to work with my cousin in construction. This made me happy. He was finally out of the house and being productive. Things were looking up.
He was not giving me a hard time. His first visit came and went. He passed the urine test. The second visit came and went. He passed it again.
I was no longer going to the doctor with him. He was on his own.
Everything seemed to be going smoothly.
He said he felt amazing.
He said the Suboxone was all he needed.
He said he did not crave the painkillers anymore.
All was great until I got a call from my cousin.

Summer of Hell (Darkness-17)
Anecdote 17

"What's going on?
My cousin rarely called me unless it was an emergency.
"Nothing, what's the matter?"
I knew immediately that he didn't call to shoot the breeze.
And he was always so blunt and to the point. Never any small talk with him.
"Yeah, listen you have to go pick up your husband at the hospital.
He fell off a ladder at work. I'll wait for you."
"What?"
Of course that was my question. He repeated himself.
"You have to pick up your husband at the hospital. He probably broke his foot. I'll wait for you."
"How? What hospital? Is he ok?"
Summer vacation was just about to start. I looked forward to summer vacation. I could finally be human. This was the first year that the kids would go to camp for a full day and the first time in a long time he finally got off the couch and went to work every day. It had been "go to work and come straight home" for me for a long time.
I never went out. Never. If I did, it was only with him and the kids. I never went out without them. I couldn't. I couldn't leave the kids alone with him anymore.
I stopped doing that years ago. Not because I feared he'd hurt them but I feared he'd make the wrong decision. So this summer was going to be about me.
I had a summer planned with nothing but *me* time. It had been a long time coming. As I was driving, I started to think and for the first time, I couldn't help but think of me.
What the hell did he do this time? I had babysat him for years. Yes, babysat him.
I'm so sick of worrying about him all the time. My life was consumed of him.

My summer was officially ruined. This was going to be an absolute nightmare.

With injury comes pain and with pain comes pills and with pills comes withdrawals and with withdrawals comes the whole cycle of bullshit once again.

This was just too much to handle. I was just so sick of the bullshit.

I couldn't help but think that this wasn't exactly an accident. Maybe he did this on purpose. Did he do this just so he could go right back to taking his pills?

I seriously had doubts.

I got to the hospital and a part of me was so angry. How will he go to work now with a broken foot. He finally gets a job and he f****d it up. This is going to suck the life out of me.

I got to the hospital and he was actually waiting outside. He was on crutches. A part of me felt bad, but the other part felt like he was full of shit. I wanted to believe him. I wanted to feel sorry for him, but I couldn't anymore.

"What in the world happened?"

"I was going up onto the roof and I just lost my footing and fell. I fell like 20 ft. It was crazy."

"20 feet? You are so lucky nothing else happened."

He didn't break it, but fractured it. But I knew. I knew he would milk this. He actually looked like he was happy about it. He wasn't upset. He wasn't mad.

He didn't look like he was in any pain. It was so weird. And that was because they gave him a painkiller. That's right, a painkiller. To anyone else, that would have been just fine, but not for him.

"You can't take painkillers! What were you thinking? What about the Suboxone?"

"I had to. I fell 20 ft. Do you know how much pain I'll be in after this wears off?"

I was so disappointed at this point. We didn't say much in the car ride home.

When we got home he went straight to lay down. I guess the high from the pills was wearing off.

I called my cousin from the other room to find out
what happened.
*"There's no way he felt that fall.There's no way. Anyone
else would not have been able to get up from a fall
like that."*
"How could he not feel it?'
*"He was high as hell before he climbed up that ladder
Claudia, that's why."*
High as hell. How could he be high as hell?
He was detoxing. I am so enraged.
An entire summer of babysitting,
an entire summer of searching for pills,
an entire summer of absolute hell lies ahead.
So here I am alone in a prison with this man
This man I can now call a liar,
a stranger,
an addict.

The Couch (Darkness-18)
Anecdote 18

"*Where are you going?*"
"*I'll be back.*"
There was no way I was going to sit around and watch him lay down all day.
I couldn't do it. I'd go crazy. He didn't have to lay around either. He could go out.
He could even drive if he wanted to.
Days and nights went by and he continued to lay on the couch. It killed me. It was eating away at me. The kids would hang out with him on the couch. He'd eat lunch and dinner on the couch. He watched endless movies on that couch.
I hated that couch. I resented that couch.
I told him after a week that he was going back on the Suboxone. I didn't want to hear any more nonsense. It was just a fracture after all.
I couldn't imagine that he'd be in continuous pain after a whole week. So just one week.
That's all I'm giving him. Then it's time to get off that couch.
I picked up the kids from camp one afternoon and when I got home, I noticed that he was more lethargic than usual. He didn't really wake up much even when the kids jumped on him. He would intermittently wake up and say random things, but I didn't really pay much attention. I chalked it up as he was sleep talking.
This continued the next day, only this time as he slept, he would make odd gestures with his arms. He'd raise them in the air and circle them around in such a peculiar way.
I'd never seen this before. It was as if he were awake and having a conversation with someone only he was using his arms to gesture. I couldn't really explain it.
I figured I'd just let him sleep.
"*They are on the hills General. Proceed on to lower grounds.*"

I jumped out of my chair. I heard him from the living room.
I nudged him, but he was wide awake.
"What are you talking about?"
"General, sir, I'm fighting for the soldiers in the Civil War."
He was hallucinating. I knew right away. It wasn't the same
high as a painkiller high.
This was different. I was able to tell the difference now.
He continued with the arm gestures. I was sick to
my stomach.
"What's wrong with daddy?"
"He's just being silly."
There was nothing anyone could do. Nothing I could do but
to wait this out.
I figured it was the perfect time to start searching. It didn't
take me long though.
I found the bottle of pills. I also found patches. I had no
idea what these patches were.
All of this was prescribed by his doctor. The one that was
notified of his rehab treatment.
The one that knew he had a drug problem.
I looked at the patches again.
Fentanyl, what the hell was that? I googled it.
*Fentanyl: is a powerful synthetic opioid analgesic that is similar
to morphine but is 50 to 100 times more potent. This medication
is used to help relieve severe ongoing pain; such as due to cancer.
Fentanyl belongs to a class of drugs known as opioid analgesics.
It works in the brain to change how your body feels and
responds to pain.*
*Do not use the patch form of fentanyl to relieve pain that is mild
or that will go away in a few days. This medication is not for
occasional "as needed" use. High doses of opioids, especially potent opioids such as fentanyl, can cause breathing to stop completely, which can lead to death.*
Holy shit. Holy shit. My heart starts racing. My hands start
shaking once again. I read it again. Maybe I read it wrong.

My eyes could only see:

50 to 100 times more potent than morphine. Given to cancer patients.

My brain could only retain:

50 to 100 times more potent than morphine. Given to cancer patients.

Wait, this doctor was giving him this potent medicine that is used in cancer patients. What the f**k for?

I'm livid.

I'm angry.

I'm fuming.

I'm a whirlwind of emotions.

It's time.

It's time I go meet this doctor.

This doctor that he loved so much.

The Appointment (Darkness-19)
Anecdote 19

"Get up! Seriously get up. You're not laying down anymore. You drove to the doctor, didn't you? You couldn't get up from this couch, but you found your way to the doctor. Where is it? Where did you put this Fentanyl patch?"

"Why?" He sort of raised his voice.

"I'm telling you right now. Take it off. You're losing your mind. Take it off right now. Did you know you thought you were in the Civil War?"

"What, really, no way."

Of course he didn't remember. He was high. There were many times he did not remember. Many. I guess that's part of being an addict. They don't remember, but their family sure will never forget.

I tried so hard to separate the kids from all of this. I tried so hard to mask them from all this. I think I had done a good job so far. I'm just so thankful that my kids were too young to understand.

He showed me his foot. The patch was placed on the top of his foot.

Today, I would not have it. Today, I was not giving in. I've gotten stronger.

*"Rip it off! Rip the f***n thing off! You will never use it again. Do you hear me? Do you know it's mainly used for cancer patients, Cancer patients! Do you have cancer? Answer me. No, no you don't. You have a fracture. It's just a fracture!"*

I was definitely yelling. He was definitely listening. He was wide awake now.

"And do you know that you are supposed to be monitored when you use fentanyl? Do you know that if the kids touched it could be lethal to them? You just don't care what you take. Whatever the hell this doctor gives you, you just take. You will never bring that shit in this house again. You will never bring this shit around our children

ever again. I don't care what your stupid doctor tells you.
Do you hear me? GET IT OFF!"
And he did. He took it off and threw it in the garbage along with the rest of the patches.

I took the garbage bag outside. I couldn't believe he listened. It was always a fight, but this time he listened. This time he knew that he was dealing with an unpredictable medicine. Medicine that he did not need.

Medicine that he knew nothing about. That doctor didn't sit him down and go over the precautions or side effects with him. He just gave it to him.

And he just got sucked right in. Doctor knows best right?

I drove to my appointment. The appointment with his loving doctor. I did not tell him where I was going.

"Hi, I'm here for an appointment."

"The doctor will be right with you."

I couldn't wait to meet this man. I would not hold back. I was just going to tell him.

I waited. And I waited. There were so many people in this office. But there was only one main doctor. Him.

Two hours went by and I finally got moved into a room.

I still waited. Finally he showed.

"Hi, I'm Dr. B."

"Hi, I'm Mrs. Marra. My husband is a patient of yours. You have been treating his fractured foot."

"Oh it's finally nice to meet you. He's such a great guy. I heard he's a great cook too.

How's his foot doing? I'm sure it's very painful?"

Is he kidding? He's a grown man with a fractured foot. Stop babying him.

And I am not here for small talk.

"Nice to finally meet you as well. Well, his foot is absolutely fine. It's his mind that worries me. He doesn't need these pain meds anymore. I do not want you giving them to him anymore. He's fine. Last night he was delirious."

"What do you mean?"

"I can't deal with him. I never know what's coming next. He gets enraged quickly.

He sleeps all the time. He's losing his mind. He won't get off the couch. He does not need medication."
"Oh no that's not the meds, that's just him being Italian."
He chuckled. He actually chuckled.
I didn't chuckle. I didn't flinch.
I can't believe this doctor just said that. And he said it with a smile.
"No, it's the pain meds you keep putting him on. He hallucinates. He doesn't know how to take them. What don't you get? You know he is on Suboxone. We need to get him off of whatever you put him on and back onto Suboxone. He's addicted. I'm telling you he is a mess."
"Well, let's see how he does with his foot. I will see him in a few days."
He wasn't going to stop giving him pills. He wasn't going to listen to me.
He wasn't going to break his doctor-patient obligation and confidentiality bullshit.
I was just the stupid wife.
I knew right then and right there that he had a bond with this doctor.
An unbreakable bond.
And I feared this bond.
I feared this bond
more than I feared
anything in the world.

Frozen (Darkness-20)

Anecdote 20

I ran to the supermarket to grab some groceries.
I always made sure a good dinner was on the table.
He never ate with us anymore. He was now a late night snacker. He would eat after midnight since he slept mostly during the day.
I always woke up when I heard him in the kitchen, fearing that he would light the stove and forget to shut it off or fearing he would use the toaster, go back to sleep and then forget it was on. Some nights, I would wake up in a panic. I would smell the burning of toast throughout the house and I'd have to get up and check on him.
I could never trust him anymore. I didn't remember the last time I had a good night sleep. It had been years.
I grabbed what I needed at the supermarket and went to the checkout. I never had an issue with my debit card. My sanity and saving grace was my job.
I was so thankful for my job. We never splurged any more though. We couldn't.
Sometimes, my parents had to help us pay our monthly bills and some months we were able to manage. It all depended on if he worked or not. I wasn't used to this.
I wasn't used to not buying what I wanted. Now it was buying only what we needed.
I went to swipe my card. *Declined*. I tried to swipe it again. *Declined*.
I left the store. No groceries in hand. I went to call the bank to fix this mistake.
"Sorry Mrs. Marra, your account has been frozen."
"Frozen, what do you mean frozen? This must be a mistake."
I had always worked. I never had money problems. My debit card was never declined.
"Why is it frozen?"

"There's a judgement against a Mr. Marra. I have the name of the lawyer who placed the freeze on the account. Do you want it? I hope this helps."

"Helps, this doesn't help. I never even heard of judgements. They can freeze your account?"

The only thing that had kept me sane while going through all of this crap was we had a roof over our head and I had good money coming in. At this point though, we were living paycheck to paycheck. But now this, this frozen account saga, was going to put me over the edge. All our money was in that account and I couldn't even buy food for our kids.

This is not what I planned for us. This is not what I signed up for.

We had hit rock bottom. Our account was frozen.

Never in a million years would I ever think that our account would have been frozen.

What the hell did he do now? Could I handle what was coming?

"Our account is frozen."

"No it's not."

"Yes, it is! Yes it is!

"How is that possible?"

"You have a judgement against you. A judgement. Why would you have a judgement against you?"

"I don't know."

"I can't take out any money. I can't take out a dime."

I gave him the number of the lawyer.

"You better figure this out."

He called the law office.

His cousin had placed a judgement against him for borrowing money.

I took a breath. I took a real long deep breath.

"How much did you borrow?"

"$25,000."

Every horrible moment that he had put me through just came back to me ten fold.

My mind was having a flashback after a flashback. I could no longer hold back.

I refused to hold back.

"*$25,000?*" I didn't even know what to say.

"*$25,000. When? When did you borrow this? I never saw a dime of that $25,000.*

What did you possibly need it for?"

He raised his voice. He didn't really have an answer. I guess he didn't want me to question him.

"*We live paycheck to paycheck and you had $25,000 to play with?*

What did you do with it? Why? Why? You spent it?"

This was one of two judgements that he had against him. One followed immediately after this one.

I knew nothing about either one. Nothing.

Drugs are evil.

Now I'm living in a prison
with a drug addict,
a stranger,
a liar,
a sneak,
And now we're pretty much broke.

Plan B (Darkness-21)
Anecdote-21

Today must have been a good day for him.
He went out.Where he went I have no idea.
But I didn't worry as much anymore. I took him off of our
main bank account and gave him a separate debit card
that only I had access to.
This made me worry less. Without money, he couldn't go to
the doctor as much to get his pills.
And to be honest, I could no longer trust him with our
money. I told him straight out why.
*"I'm no longer letting you have access to our bank account.
I work my ass off. You take money out and I never know
what you need it for. When I ask you, you get nasty. And
you're definitely buying pills with it. I know it. We are on a
budget now. Not because of me but because of you."*
I couldn't have him take food out of our own children's
mouths. He knew. He knew at this point that he had hit
rock bottom. He totally understood.
*"I'll put some money in your account if you want to buy
food or gas. And that will be it."*
How sad that it has come down to this? We had everything. Everything.
And now it was almost down to nothing.
I had to do this. I didn't want to. No man wants this, but if I
was going to save him, this was a step in the right
direction.
Things had gotten bad. Really bad on so many levels. On
every level. He went through thousands. Hundreds of
thousands of dollars.
Money was an issue. He even had to ask his parents for a
loan to pay off the $25,000 so they could unfreeze our ac-
count. My parents had already helped us financially in so
many ways. I could never repay them.
And we were already on a budget but now add on that I
had to pay this loan that his parents took out for him,

every month.

My next step was to call the rehab center.

The only hope I had left. The only hope he had left.

I had to let them know that he was back on his pills and that his doctor is continuing to prescribe them for him. I needed a game plan and I was hoping the doctor could help me.

"Hi, may I speak to Dr. S. It's Mrs. Marra?"

"Please hold."

"Hi Mrs. Marra. How are you?"

"Not doing well. How are you? I'm calling about my husband's next visit with you. We need a new game plan. He is back to his old tricks again and back on pain medication. So if he tries to come there for Suboxone. Don't give it to him. He's abusing it. We need a plan B."

"Mrs. Marra, I was meaning to call you."

Here it comes. Here comes the news I was not hoping for but knew was coming.

"Your husband got kicked out of the program many weeks ago."

"What?"

This seems to be the infamous question lately.

"We tested him and he came up positive for hydrocodone. We had no choice.

This was actually the second time he tested positive. He was already let go.

I'm so sorry."

"Wait, but why didn't you tell me? I signed the contract with him. You were to let me know."

"Sorry Mrs. Mar......"

I hung up before he could finish.

This is not what I wanted for me. This is not what I wanted for us. This is not what I wanted for our kids.

I had to face it.
I was married to a drug addict
and nobody,
nobody, could help us.
I was numb.

Job Hunting (Darkness-22)

Anecdote 22

He tried to open up a painting business.
I even made business cards for him and flyers. I tried to support him even after all he put me through. I knew the best thing to do was leave him. But he was the father of my children and I knew he would be so lost without his kids. There wouldn't have been any chance of him getting clean then. I thought that me leaving him would really push him over the edge.
And the kids were so little. They still needed him. I wanted them to be proud of him.
I was thrilled that he started to get himself out there. He was finally seeing the bigger picture. We needed money. He was gung-ho at first. My mother even gave him $3,000 to help him start the new business up. She only wanted the best for all of us.
He picked up a few jobs. He was going strong at first. He got a few jobs and then before you knew it, it plummeted. It wasn't even a few weeks and he was leaving his workers to paint and he would head back home to the couch once again.
It was a loss. A complete loss and a complete waste of time.
I told him he needed to work for someone even if it was waiting tables at this point. He wasn't capable of handling a business. No way was he capable.
He had to go out there and find a job. There definitely were times when he functioned. He was very able to find a job. Keeping it was another story. I'd call him every day from work to make sure he was job hunting.
"Did you look for anything today?"
"There was nothing."
"You have to try tomorrow then."

My mother and father helped us out a lot until we could get back on our feet.

Until we could figure this all out. Even my sister helped me out. I hadn't a clue when we'd get back on our feet, but knowing they were there for me and the kids was a blessing. They all knew what was going on.

There was no hiding it. They just never really knew the daily struggles of what living with him were. I didn't have the heart to tell them. They would have been too worried. I tried to handle so much on my own.

My mom would come every Sunday to check on us and buy us whatever we needed. From groceries to whatever toys the boys wanted. The kids really didn't miss out on anything. They were definitely spoiled by my parents.

My mother knew a lot of people through her campaigning for politicians in our town.

She would always keep her eyes and ears open for job opportunities for him. Weeks went by and she finally heard of something. It couldn't have come at a better time.

"Ok I got the perfect job for him."

My mom knew a woman who used to always come to our restaurant. She remembered us. She remembered him. She loved him.

"What job? Where?"

"I got him an interview to be a Nassau County Inspector. It's a really good job."

"Really? Wow. That's incredible. He will be so happy."

This is it. This is what he needed. A good job. A union job. Things were going to get better. He was thrilled about the news. He was actually looking forward to it. I think he had finally woken up.

I couldn't have been happier either.

Wow, things were going to be okay.

It was October.
He did get the job.
The only problem was the job didn't start
until February.
And there was a long time in between now and then
to keep an addict busy.
A really ,
really long time.

The Bathtub (Darkness-23)
Anecdote 23

One of my best friends was getting married. I had never left my kids since things had gotten so bad with him, but I had to go to this. Even for an hour.
There was no way he was coming with me either. In a way, we weren't really a couple anymore. We were still married, yes, but his addiction had taken over every aspect of our life. There was no more romance or date nights.
That was long gone.
On the day of the wedding he seemed down and depressed.
I knew this would happen. I had called his mother earlier though in the week to stay with the kids and
him while I was at the wedding. There was no way I would leave them alone with him for a whole night. I figured she could spend time with her son and enjoy her grandchildren too. Normally though and it had happened several times, I would have said, "Sorry, I can't make it, something came up", but I just couldn't make up excuses anymore. All I did was make up excuses.
This was an important day for my friend and I needed to be there. I figured they would be fine especially since their grandmother would be there.
I didn't intend to stay long.
I got ready and waited for his mother to show up.
My stomach was in knots. I did not want to leave. I had to drive to the other side of the island. This made it worse.This was going to be so hard for me, but I did it.
This was the first time in years that I left my house for the night without my kids.
The wedding was beautiful. I missed the beginning though. I had gotten there a little late.
I called home to check in and his mother answered.
"Hello."

"Hi, is all ok there?"
"Yes, all good. I brought homemade pizza for everyone."
"Did the kids eat?"
"Yes."
"How is he?"
"He's good. We're laughing with the kids."
Great. All is good home. I can relax a little. I was so fidgety at the table though.

I knew people were looking at me, but I couldn't help it. I kept looking at my phone. I was definitely scarred by all of this. Nobody knew what I was going through.

I didn't tell anyone except some of my family and my best friend. His family knew too.

I called home again about 45 minutes later.

Nobody picked up.

I gave them another 15 minutes and he picked up. I couldn't understand what he was saying. I told him to get Luca on the phone.

"Hi sweetie. Where's Nonna?"
"She left."
She was not supposed to leave until I got home.
"She left? When?"
"A little while ago."
"Are you okay? "
"Yes."
I didn't want to scare him. He was my world.
"Get ready for bed sweetie. Mommy will be home in 45 minutes."
"Mommy."
"Yes, my love."
"Daddy fell in the bathtub, but don't worry he got up."
Did he just say Daddy fell in the bathtub?

I grabbed my pocketbook and I ran out of that catering hall so fast. No goodbyes. No nothing.

I raced home. This man was going to be the death of me. I got home in record time.

I opened the door.

The kids greeted me in their pajamas with big smiles on their faces. I was so relieved to see them and their smiles. They were such good kids. They never gave me a hard time. I held their hands, gave them big kisses and I put them to sleep in my bed.

I went to the bathroom. I saw exactly what Luca told me on the phone. I saw the shower curtain and the rod. They were at the bottom of the bathtub.

He really did fall into the bathtub.

My question was:

How?

My next question was:

Why?

I go to the den and there he was, curled up in a fetal position, passed out. Not a care in the world.

And that was the last time,
the very last time,
I ever left the house at night,
And sadly that was the last time,
the very last time.
I ever left my kids alone with a man
who they call their dad.
Ever.

The New Job (Darkness-24)
Anecdote 24

I begged him to go to rehab. Begged him. Several times actually. He didn't think he was that bad. Addicts never admit they have a problem. Addicts lie.
Addicts hold secrets. They just know that rehab meant you are no longer able to get high. An addict will never go to rehab unless they are willing to go and he was not willing to go, especially now that he got a new job.
Months passed and although it was hell, today was the day. Today was the day he started his new job. I got through the past three months just knowing that there were brighter days ahead. It wasn't easy. Believe me, it wasn't easy.
He went out and bought a few new shirts. He got a haircut too. He seemed pretty excited to start.
You have no idea how excited I was. This is what he needed. He had to feel important again. He had to feel like a man again.
I owed my mom so much already, but this time she really pulled through. By having the two of us working, we were sure to be okay. At least when it came to finances.
I had hired a great girl to get the kids on and off the bus. I didn't want him to have any stress. I didn't want him to make any excuses. He just could not screw this up.
If it were up to him, he'd stay home just so he could put the kids on the bus and stay on the couch. She was my friend's daughter. I didn't make many friends in this new neighborhood, but this family was just like mine. I was so happy she took the job. The kids loved her and I could trust her. Things were looking up.
I was nervous all day. I was hoping that he made it through day one without any problems, without any excuses, and without any episodes.

I called him during lunch.
"How's it going?"
"Good. This job is so easy."
"They're even giving me a car."
"A car?"
"Yes, I have to drive to different places to inspect buildings."
'That's great. How are the people there?"
"They are so cool. I have a partner too. He's training me this week."
"Wow, I'm so happy to hear. See, this is what you needed."
"Yeah, I like it so far."
I practically danced my way through the rest of the day. I was elated. I figured if we got our finances together that he would begin to straighten out, step by step. He will finally feel whole again. He will have a reason to get off that couch that I hated so much.
Who I felt the the happiest for though were our boys. I wanted their daddy to get clean for them. They won't see it now, nor did they understand, but later they will. It was so important to get clean for his children.
I pulled up from work. I was a little nervous. The kids ran to me. They loved their new babysitter and she loved them. I was so relieved. I booked her for the whole week and into the next and the next. I may have gotten ahead of myself. I cooked some dinner for us. I figured we would eat together as a family for once.
I knew he would get home around 5:00. There weren't going to be any surprises.
And he did. He got home on time. We ate dinner together. He seemed like he was good. Really good actually. He interacted with the kids. He didn't fall asleep on the couch that night until we all went to sleep. That was a first.
I couldn't believe it. This was so good for the kids.
A week went by and then almost another week. He continued to go to work.
He liked his partner and his partner felt the same.

He'd tell me stories about the places they had to inspect each day. It seemed like a pretty cool job.

Things were falling back into place.

He made it through yet another week and I couldn't believe it was going to be Friday once again. This made two full weeks of work for him.

This weekend was going to be great. He had an event to go to with the kids. He promised them. We had bought Max WWE tickets for his birthday back in July.

Both of our boys were WWE fanatics. We surprised him. He wanted to go so badly. I made sure to buy the tickets way in advance. We had bought a WWE figurine and we taped the tickets to the back of it. The look on Max's face was priceless when he realized they were tickets to see WWE Raw. I loved moments like that.

Our kids meant the world to us.

Friday morning came and the kids were definitely so excited to go with their dad.

We went off to work. The day went by so fast.

I didn't hear from him at all that day so I figured all was good.

I pulled up to the house.

I saw his car in the driveway. I thought that was strange. He was home pretty early.

They didn't have to leave until 7:00.

I walked in and the kids ran up to me. They were so excited, exceptionally excited.

I was so curious to find out where he was. I didn't have to look far. He was in the bedroom, in bed.

But he wasn't sleeping.

This was such bullshit. If I could have screamed F**K as loud I could at the very moment, I would have.

"What's wrong?"

"I didn't feel good. I thought I was having a heart attack."

"What do you mean having a heart attack? What happened? You left work?"

"I went to the doctor during lunch, then my boss made me go home."

Oh my God. Oh my God. This wasn't happening. This wasn't actually happening.
Every hope I had
was just crushed.
Every hope I had for our kids
just crumbled before me.
And there were our boys with their WWE shirts on,
my beautiful boys,
in the entrance of our bedroom,
with disappointment on their face
and tears in their eyes.

WWE (Darkness-25)

Anecdote 25

"I don't think I can take them tonight. My doctor said my blood pressure was too high and he put me on medicine. I seriously thought I was having a heart attack."
"Your doctor? When did you go see him? You were working?"
What doesn't he get? What doesn't he see? His blood pressure was high because all of the pills he swallows. He just loved going to see his doctor. His cure for all.
It was so weird. He was smiling at me. He was smiling a lot. I thought he said he wasn't feeling well, but it didn't seem like it.
I wasn't going to let him drive them tonight. I was going to drop them off. All of them. He was no longer allowed to drive our kids around. I made that decision a long time ago. He didn't agree with it, but he didn't argue either. But tonight and every day forward I would be driving.
I looked over onto the night table. And there they were. An orange bottle of pills.
I hated the color orange.
He never left pills in sight. Never. So strange.
"Mommy, we can't go? Please, please, can you take us?"
Max started to cry. I couldn't take it.
There was no way I was disappointing my babies.
"Of course mommy will take you."
They were so excited.
I didn't like the way he was acting though. Something was just so off.
His high tonight wasn't the same. It didn't make him as lethargic. At least not yet.
His high tonight made him very alert. His eyes were bright and wide. He had such a weird smirk on his face. I couldn't figure it out. I had to get my hands on those pills.
I needed to see what this doctor prescribed him.

I waited until he fell asleep. I knew he'd fall asleep at some point.I took the entire bottle of pills and took them with me. I counted them.

So many were gone already. He had just picked them up from the pharmacy. Unbelievable. He was at the point of his addiction where he could no longer make logical decisions. Everything was impulsive. Everything was unpredictable.

Everything was wrong.

Bottom line was I had to take my boys tonight. I had to. But how could I leave him? Something just wasn't right and to boot he took more than he was supposed to. The reality of all this was he was an addict after all.

The doctor knew that. I had already warned him.

I checked the pill bottle. His doctor put him on Ativan. I never heard of it.

I wasn't familiar with any of these pills that this doctor prescribed. I had a feeling he was going through a withdrawal and knew his doctor would prescribe him something.

Sometimes when he was going through a withdrawal he would drink an entire bottle of Robitussin. I guess this time that wasn't his plan. So his doctor prescribed an addict, an addict going through a withdrawal, Ativan.

Ativan: Is a controlled substance.It can treat seizure disorders, such as epilepsy.It can also be used before surgery and medical procedures to relieve anxiety. Can cause paranoid or suicidal ideation and impair memory, judgment, and coordination. Combining with other substances, particularly alcohol, can slow breathing and possibly lead to death.

Ativan is highly addictive. For this reason, prescribing doctors should inquire with patients about their history of drug abuse, if any, or whether addiction issues are common in their families. Studies show that when Ativan and Xanax are used for more than one month, dependence will occur in 47% of those taking them.

That's great. So now he is prescribing him Ativan on top of Xanax and hydrocodone.

And this is only what I know of.

Everything this doctor prescribed to him for some reason could lead to death.

Everything that this doctor prescribed to him was highly addictive.

Ativan, with a combination of what he had already prescribed him, was disastrous.

I can't take this asshole of a doctor. He had no concern with his abusive history nor did he have any concern for his well being. None.

Now, I was torn between babysitting him or taking our kids to WWE and I knew I had to take them. There was no way I would break their hearts.

I had already taken the rest of his Ativan away, so I figured he would just stay asleep for the night. My kids hadn't been to a fun event like this in a while.

They deserved to go. I figured I would just check in on him a little later.

It sadly wasn't my first rodeo with him, so I knew he would just sleep it off.

And off we went.

I was so happy to be there with my kids.
but as I was sitting there,
something just wasn't sitting right.
Something just wasn't right at all.
I began to breathe heavy.
Panic set in as I
began to dial his cell.

The Tree (Darkness-26)

Anecdote 26

I called to check in with him but he didn't answer.
I waited until about 8:15 to call again. No answer. Something just wasn't right.
Something in my gut felt that something was wrong. So very wrong.
I know there were several times he didn't answer his phone, believe me I knew, but tonight was different. I couldn't explain it. I gave the kids a few more minutes and then grabbed them to leave.
During the car ride, we talked about the few WWE fighters that they saw. They were so cute.
We were almost home by the end of our conversation. I wish that I could have frozen time. We had just gotten onto Peninsula Blvd.
I just knew something was wrong. But exactly what, I couldn't figure it out.
As I approached our street, I saw flashes of reds and blues. It was like the sky lit up in just those colors, red and blue. I slowed down. As I got closer, I saw the police lights. I saw several police cars. I went into panic mode. I thought I was having a panic attack. I never had one before, but I for sure was having one then. I was at a complete stop now.
There were several police cars surrounding a tree. It looked like a crime scene. And there it was. There was a car that looked just like his wrapped around a tree.
It looked like an accordion. It must have just happened. That person could not still be alive. They crashed head on right into a tree. A huge tree. A monstrous tree.
You could barely see the front of their car anymore. It was now embedded.
I was talking myself out of it. It just can't be. It couldn't be. Was I seeing it right?
Could it be his car? It can't be.

Then, I started to scream. I started to cry. Then, I started to pray. I prayed out loud. I prayed that it wasn't him. I kept praying out loud.

"Please don't be daddy. Please God, don't let it be him."

My poor kids. For the first time, I made them afraid. I made them terrified.

I was praying out loud. I couldn't contain myself. I couldn't, for the first time, be strong for my kids.

"Please be home when we get there. Please, please, please be home."

"Mommy what's wrong?"

I didn't answer. I couldn't be strong for them. I couldn't answer.

We pulled up and his car was no longer in the driveway. It was him. That car. That car that hit the tree, that car that hit the monstrous tree, the car that was embedded into the tree, was his.

"OH MY GOD! OH MY GOD!"

I couldn't breathe. I began to hyperventilate.

I ran inside with the kids.

He was nowhere to be found. He wasn't there.

His wallet and cell phone were on the floor of our bedroom. He wouldn't leave without his wallet or cell phone.

Why did he drop his wallet and cellphone?

I called his family to come watch the kids. I called his brother too. I needed to go to the scene. I just couldn't do it alone.

"We have to go. We have to go now. He crashed into a tree. A tree. There's no way he made it. There's no way."

"Ok. Ok. Are you sure? I'll be right there."

I fell to the ground. I fell right to the ground. Right on my knees.

My poor babies. I have sheltered them and protected them for so long from all his shit. But tonight, tonight I fell apart.

"Mommy is he going to be okay?"

I prayed out loud again.

I took a deep breath.

I took another deep breath. My poor Luca had to lend me his hand just so I could get enough balance to get up. I was so sorry that they both had to see me like this.

"Yes baby. Mommy is going to check on daddy right now. I'm sure he is fine. I promise."

I promised?

I made a promise to my innocent son

that I knew was a lie.

Their father wasn't fine.

Their father wasn't fine at all.

I think their father may have died tonight.

His Trunk (Darkness-27)
Anecdote 27

"Go, go, go. It's right there. Around the corner."
You couldn't miss this scene. It looked like it came right from a movie.
The tires screeched as we pulled up.
His brother barely put the car in park. I started to scream. I was so scared. I ran out. He ran out. Our doors left wide open right on Peninsula Blvd.
"What happened? Where is he?"
"M'am who are you?"
"I'm his wife."
"The man in this car was taken to the hospital already."
"Is he okay?"
"All I can tell you is he was just taken to the hospital."
The car was totaled. It was so surreal to see it up close. The front of the car was no longer. Two telephone poles were knocked down. Ripped right out of the ground. It looked like a tornado hit. He knocked down two telephone poles. This can't be happening.
What was he thinking? What was he doing? And where the hell was he going?
It was the very moment at the WWE event when I felt sick to my stomach that he hit this tree. I felt it.
I just stood there in utter silence. Looking at the disaster that he left behind him.
All I could think about were my boys. My precious boys.
The cop on the scene pulled me aside and whispered to me.
"M'am was this your husband?"
"Yes."
"Do you have children?"
I just started to cry.
"Yes."
"Please listen to me then. And listen to me good. He was driving under the influence. He refused a breathalyzer. I've

never seen anything like this and your husband was way over the limit. We had to use the jaws of life to pry him out. And from what witnesses saw, he was speeding, zig zagging in and out of traffic. He went onto the curb a few times, hitting telephone poles and other trees. Then he finally hit this tree. He was definitely speeding at a very high speed. Had to be going 50 or 60 when he hit the tree."

"I don't even know what to say."

"You need to get your husband help. He had no idea what he was doing."

"I know. I know."

"He should have died here tonight. He could have killed people here tonight. He could've killed himself."

He brought me to his trunk. Th trunk was still in tact.

"Here, come with me."

He opened his trunk.

I couldn't believe my eyes.

"I found a lot of pills in his trunk. Some were in bottles with prescriptions. Some were not."

Oh my God. His trunk. He used his trunk for his stash.

"Holy shit."

"It seems that he was on a lot of different pills tonight. He tried to tell me he has scripts for all of these, but I highly doubt it."

I knew from our conversation though that he made it out alive.

Tonight he thought he was unstoppable. Untouchable.
Where was he going?
And does he even know of the disaster he had left behind?
Welcome to my life of living with an addict.
I didn't know the extent of his injuries,
but I knew that tonight,
tonight,
I didn't have to tell my boys that their father died.

Handcuffed (Darkness-28)

Anecdote 28

We drove to the hospital. We were both just in awe. We had no idea what was in store for us when we saw him. We had questions. So many questions.
I thought the worst. The very worst.
We ran into the entrance of the hospital.
We get to the ER and they directed us to his room.
And there he was just sitting there in the hospital bed.
And there he was with just minor cuts and bruises.
And there he was surrounded by cops.
And there he was f***king handcuffed, handcuffed to his bed.
I almost fainted. Handcuffed?
I didn't say a word. I couldn't even look at him. My life and my sons' lives had just changed dramatically because of this man. This man that I decided to marry and spend the rest of my life with. This man who is now in handcuffs. Who is now a criminal.
My life would never be the same.
My sons' father was now a criminal.
I was a good person. I always took care of my family. I always went to work.
I never called in sick. I never had an issue with the law. Until now.
His brother did all the talking.
I just observed.
"I don't remember."
"Try to. Trace back your steps. Did you call anyone? Where were you going?"
"I think I blacked out. I wasn't feeling good earlier. I may have been driving myself to the hospital."
I interrupted.
"No, you blacked out because you were high. You were high as hell and that's why you don't remember."

I said it right in front of the cops. The same cop that pulled me aside was there now, too.

"Your car is totaled. You hit a tree. You took down telephone poles."

"I don't remember."

"How do you not remember?"

Ativan: can cause impaired memory, judgment, and coordination.

I'm sure driving was not permitted while on Ativan.

"What did you take? How many did you take?"

At this point, he was under investigation. We couldn't say much more.

"The judge is going to be here in the morning to arraign him and set a court date."

Arraign him? I was in awe.

I had nothing else to say to him.

His brother and I waited in the waiting room for quite some time after. We had a long talk.

We were useless there.

I did say goodbye, but that was about it.

It was about 5 a.m when I walked in the door.

I looked on the computer for a lawyer and I called him.

A lawyer that specialized in DUI's. With lawyers came money. Money we did not have.

I didn't even know what questions to ask a DUI lawyer. He did all the talking and I did the listening.

"I'll see him and the judge in the late morning."

I picked up my boys at 7 from my in laws.

I hadn't slept a wink. I didn't care.

I hugged them so tight. Luca was so worried. Max just followed whatever Luca said and did. They were too cute like that. He was the younger brother after all.

"Is Daddy okay?

"Yes, yes Daddy is fine. Didn't I tell you daddy would be fine?"

And that was the God awful truth
At least about tonight it was.
Daddy was fine for tonight.
I didn't have to break any promises.
I didn't have to lie.
A mother's strength is like no other.
A mother's strength is truly unbreakable.

Head Nurse (Darkness-29)

Anecdote 29

I called into work again. I needed two days to get every-thing under control.
It was so unlike me. But my kids needed me. They were my priority.
I dropped my kids to school that day. They didn't take the bus. I wanted to spend as much time with them as I could before they went to school. Luca was in second grade and Max was in first grade. They were at great ages.
I loved being with them.
After I dropped them, I just wanted to cry. I wanted to break down and cry for them.
My heart broke for them and they didn't even know why.
I went through hell last night. You could see it all over my face.
I had dropped so much weight since things had gotten bad. I never wanted to eat. I was always so sick to my stomach. I was at a very unhealthy weight. People at work were worried about me even though they didn't know what was going on.
It was terrible, but I had to keep going.
Today was going to be hard. Today I had to visit him in the hospital. I didn't want to talk to him.
The lawyer called me. His court date was set for next week. They were giving him time since he hadn't been released from the hospital yet.
He also told me that he lost his license until then and may lose it for up to 6 months to a year.
The lawyer knew how upset I was about the handcuffs. He told me they took them off. I wasn't going in until they came off. A part of me was so glad that he lost his license. He needed to be off the road. He was a danger.
I didn't know where this would leave him with his job though when he got home.

Driving as well as driving with a clean license was part of the job. He would probably now lose his position. He had only been there for two weeks.

I got to the hospital. My visit with him was very difficult. I was so angry with him.

I was so sick of being his babysitter, his nurse, his doctor, his provider, his secretary, his bail me out of jail card. Never, never was it what I originally signed up for.

I was never his wife.

I think I was still in shock. Honestly, it was like I was visiting someone at a funeral home. That hospital room was so dreary and melancholy. I was very quiet. I wanted nothing but to get home to my kids and be a mother.

The head nurse that day just came in and punched in for the night shift. She had been working the night he came in. She saw me and called me over. She had a long talk with me.

"I was here last night when your husband came in. Did anyone go over his blood work with you?

She rattled off some names of medications. I was only familiar with some of them. I just had enough at this point.

"He could have gotten discharged tomorrow, but I pushed for him to stay."

"Why are you pushing for him to stay?"

"He was begging us to give him pain medicine. We refused. He is not allowed pain medication and it is on his chart."

"Really? I figured you were obligated to give it to him."

"We usually do, but he didn't break anything and your husband has a serious pain management problem. He needs to stay here to detox. This is why I am pushing for him to stay."

"Thank you so much. I didn't think hospitals did that."

She was so nice to me.

"They really don't. This case though really hit home for me. My brother who was around this age was addicted to pills. He had a beautiful wife and a beautiful child."

"Oh, I'm sorry."

I understood now why she was pushing for his stay.
"Is he still addicted?"
I should have known where this was going.
"He died last year."
My mouth opened wide.
"What? What happened?"
"He overdosed."
My heart. My heart broke for her.
This could have been me. This could have been me last night.
"Your husband should have died last night. He is very lucky to be sitting here with us today. He told me he had two sons. He spoke so highly of them. He really loves them. His eyes lit up when he told me about them."
I just started to cry. I cried and cried. She gave me a big hug.
"Your husband will stay here for the next four days and he will detox here."
I was so thankful. I was so thankful that she cared.
We talked for about an hour. I needed her today. I really needed someone to talk to.
I went back into his room.
I spoke to him in low, firm voice, but wanted him to hear me loud and clear too.
"Once you get out of this place, you will be going to rehab. I am going to find you an in patient rehab facility where you have to live there day in an day night. I don't really care how you feel about it. Our children could have been in that car with you last night and that makes me f****ing sick. They would never have survived that crash. Honestly, I can't even look at you right now."
My children had me. I would never had allowed them to be in that car with him last night.
But It was just the thought of it. The what if. It took over my heart, my soul, my every thought.
"If you decide not to go to rehab. I am leaving you. I am taking the children with me and I am leaving.

I have had enough. Do you understand? I had just about enough of all your bullshit. It just never ends."

He looked at me and he knew I was serious.

"I heard you were asking for painkillers. Painkillers got you here. We don't deserve this life. I deserve a husband that can take care of me and take care of his family. I have supported you for so long. I always tried to help you. I never turned my back on you. I deserve my life back. Our children deserve their father back. A father who is clean. A father that can take them places. Until you decide to get clean and get your shit together, our children will not be coming here to visit you."

That was the hardest thing to say to a father, but I stuck to my word.

Our children did not go visit him.

I was done.

It was about me now.

It was about my future.

It was finally about me.

I am strong.

Kindergartner (Darkness-30)
Anecdote 30

I am a new woman. I am stronger.
I think it's time to pay his doctor another visit.
I'm pissed. I'm livid. I'm going after him.
This is my life he is hurting. These our my kids that he
is hurting.
I have to get our life back.
This doctor had contributed to his addiction. Everyone
blames the addict.
They are sometimes only half the problem.
He has made it too easy for him. He's prescribed Vicodin
and Xanax in bulk. Lithium, Methadone, Zyprexa, Ativan,
Paxil just to name a few. All prescribed to a healthy man.
It made me so sick.
Even if he tried, with this concoction of drugs, he would
never have been able to get his life back on track.
This is going to be the last time he uses his pen and pad to
destroy our family.
His pen and pad were evil. Pure evil.
The very next day I drove to the doctor's office.
No appointment. No warning.
I waltzed right over to the front desk.
"I need to see Dr.B and I need to see him now."
"Do you have an appointment?"
*"I don't have an appointment. It's not about me. I need to
speak to him on a personal level."*
They put me in a room. The doctor came in.
"Hi Mrs. Marra. How are you? What's wrong?"
I look him dead in the eyes. I never lost eye contact.
*"My husband almost killed himself last night after visiting
you. I don't know why you prescribed him what you did but
his car went right into a tree. He blacked out. If you do not
stop giving him pills, he will die and I will go after you."*
I was shaking at this point. I started to cry.
"I'm so sorry to hear that."

"I'm telling you if you do not stop giving him pills, I am going to go after you. Do you understand me? He lost his license. He got a DUI. I don't care if you are obligated to only him. I'm done with this bullshit. I am done with you. He's addicted. I know that and you know that."
He looked right at me. Shook his head.
"He's going to be discharged from the hospital soon. They have him detoxing. The very first thing he's going to do is come looking for you. He's going to come looking for his pills. And you aren't going to give him one god damn thing."
"Ok, if he comes I will not give him anything. Don't worry, I'll treat him just like a kindergartner from here on in."
Those words have been embedded in my brain.
He hands me a pain management card.
"Call them. They can help him."
"Call them, they can help him," he said. Wow, you created this mess and now someone else has to fix it.
He then proceeds to hand me a script. A script for 800 mg of Advil. Really? That was a joke.
"This should help him with the need for painkillers. Give this to him when he gets out."
He shook my hand. He knew this was serious.
I left there with a card in one hand,
a script in the other,
and those words embedded in my brain,
"I'll treat him like a kindergartner."
I'll never forget those words.
I'll never forget those words
until the day I die.

The Paper (Darkness-31)
Anecdote 31

His court date was set for next week.
His lawyer knew the judge so he thinks they may be easy on him.
If he could prove that his pills were prescribed by his doctor then he may not lose his license.
He detoxed in the hospital for four days.
Four days is not nearly enough, but it was probably the longest he had been clean in years.
I picked him up at about 11:30 Tuesday morning.
He was discharged on Advil. Just Advil.
Him being in the hospital was a well needed break for me.
For once, I didn't have to worry about where he was, what he was doing or what he was taking.
I felt relieved. It had been such a long time since I felt normal. Even though we had a long road ahead of us, it was nice to breathe again.
I know that now it'll be back to worrying again.
His court date, his job, his license, the car, the lawyer, the telephone poles, insurance.
It all needed to be taken care of.
He was lucky to leave there with only a bruised rib and a couple of cuts and bruises. He didn't even need stitches.
I still didn't have much to say to him.
He wanted to go see his car at the impound and since he no longer had a license and couldn't drive,
I had to take him.
I don't think he realized how bad his accident was.
He needed to see the car for himself. He hadn't seen it yet.
I was hoping that the car would be a wake up call for him. How could it not be?
We pull into the police impound and there it was. His car, or what was left of his car really.
"Oh my God. This is my car."
"You are so lucky."

"I can't believe it."
His eyes scanned the car from top to bottom.
I think he was in shock at first. Sadly, he really didn't remember what happened that night of the accident. Not one thing.
I took a lot of pictures. Seeing the car after the fact was incredibly difficult. I was so embarrassed that this all happened. Word started to get around already. I didn't tell anyone in my family or at work that he got arrested. I just couldn't do it.
I just couldn't yet.
They only knew he got into a bad car accident.
On the car ride home, I told him about my visit to the doctor. I wasn't holding back anymore.
"I went to see Dr.B."
"You did, why?"
"Why? You have to ask me why? I told him you were going to come visit him for pills and that he better not even think about giving you one more painkiller and if he did, I would go after him. So don't even think about going to see him."
He didn't say much. I think reality was setting in.
"I have your brother coming over to stay with you while I'm at work tomorrow. He'll keep you company. I'm also looking into in patient rehab once your court date clears. I told you that I'm serious about leaving you if you don't go."
I needed to keep a close eye on him. For some reason, I knew that this accident would be an excuse for him to get back on pain meds. Honestly,I don't think the crash or seeing the car did much for him. It seems like he knew he got out unscathed and now life will just resume as normal. I was hoping the opposite.
I mean technically, as per the cop, he should have died on that impact.
We pull into our driveway. The kids were still in school.
He missed them for sure.
He settled in and called work. They told him to take care of himself. He also needed a doctor's note in order to return.

They were so nice to him. He was fortunate that he could go back. I don't think they knew he got arrested, but at some point he had to tell them he lost his license.
I started to go through the mail. I hadn't really gone through it while he was at the hospital. I couldn't look at another bill.
"Look at this."
'What is it?"
I just stood there staring. I was in awe. It just never stops.
"What, what is it?"
He grabbed the local paper from me.
*"Oh sh*t."*
He jaw dropped and for the first time since the accident something triggered.
In an instant, his whole demeanor changed his face turned a ghastly grey.
A grey that from that point never went away.
He had made the local paper.
Yes, indeed. He made the local paper.
Accident, DUI, and all.

The Rental (Darkness-32)
Anecdote 32

The next two weeks from the moment he got home from the hospital were the most confusing, most grueling, and the most heartbreaking times of my life.
His brother had taken him to his court date.
I had to go to work.
I asked his brother to come over a lot until he recovered. Just to keep an eye on him.
He was able to produce prescriptions for the few Suboxone pills the police found that were in an unscripted bottle. The rest had scripts. The DUI charges were dropped.
He was to get his license back in a week. I couldn't believe it. I was pissed. I wanted him off the road until I got him into a rehab. I wanted him to learn a lesson.
But something happened to him within these two weeks. That ghastly grey color in his face never disappeared.
And the cane. Remember the cane he used when he broke his toe? It reappeared. He started to use the cane again. He only had a bruised rib. I didn't understand what his obsession was with this cane.
But he wasn't the same. He was like the Tasmanian Devil. It was like he got a new lease on life. He started calling people. People he hadn't spoken to in months and in years. He'd call them and tell them he loved them. He'd call them and tell them he needed to see them. He was just non stop. On the go. On the go. He rented a car while I was at work and went to visit people. They were in shock that he visited.
This was so unlike him. He was off that couch.
He went out and bought a new jacket and some new clothes. I don't know where he got money from. He started to wear a long rosary bead and this gold cross.
I'll never forget that combination. He said he felt an angel saved him the night of the accident. I guess he wanted to

be closer to God. I just couldn't figure him out. It seemed like he was a completely different person.
I caught up with him on my way home from work.
We met in the entrance.

"I have to go."

"Where are you going? I do not want you driving."

It's so hard to tell an adult what to do.

"I have to go. I have big plans."

"Listen you need to take it down a notch. You are all over the place. What's going on? You're getting me nervous. It's like your spiraling out of control. Calm down."

"Just trust me. Just trust me. Don't worry."

Don't worry he said. Now I was even more worried.
He came back pretty early. He was so alert still.
Too alert. Wide eyed alert. Heart racing alert.
We both were sitting at the dining room table.

"I found a place close by that has an in patient rehab. I called today. The nurse at the hospital gave me a few numbers on the day of your discharge. You need help. It's time."

"Ok when?"

I don't think he gets it. This is serious. He has to call. I can't do anything for him anymore.

"You have to call. They would only give me some informa-tion. The first part of rehab is you have to make the call and admit that you have a problem. It shows that you are willing to do this and that nobody forced you."

"Ok I will call tomorrow."

"Wait until I get home and we will call together. I want to be there."

The next morning came and I will never forget.
I had meetings all day so it was going to be an easy day for me. I still had this wonderful girl putting the kids on the bus and taking them off the bus. I couldn't depend on him anymore. I wouldn't.
I went into his rental car. I had to move it because it was blocking my car.

And there it was. My heart just skipped a million beats. I thought I was having another panic attack. The same feeling came over me when I saw his car embedded into a tree. The same exact feeling.
And the words came back to me. Those words that I said I will never forget.
"We'll treat him like a kindergartner."
Dr. B promised. Yes, he promised. He shook my hand and promised me. That piece of shit.
I was enraged. I was livid. I was distraught.
I was f***ing pissed.
On his passenger seat was a whole box of Fentanyl patches.Fentanyl. I was speechless. There was a box of patches. Some were already missing.
He didn't even try to hide them.
This explains his attitude. This explains his speed. This explains it all.
Holy shit he lied to me.
There was his script, right on the box written by Dr.B. in black and white letters.
I will never forget. I will never forget this morning.
I grabbed the patches and I grabbed his car keys.
And I went off to work.
With patches in one hand,
His car keys in the other,
and a feeling of pure nausea in my stomach
caused by an addict and his drug dealer.
His drug dealer, Dr.B.

Upstate (Darkness- 33)
Anecdote 33

My ride to school was typical.
At least for an addict's wife it was.
I had a 45 minute ride to school.
A place where I taught 125 amazing children.
I always greeted them with a smile and I meant it.
Besides my own children, they were all my kids too.
I owed it to them to be the energetic, positive person I was no matter how I felt inside.
Not once did I ever let them see my heartache.
And on my passenger seat on my ride to my safe place, my sanity, my normalcy were Fentanyl patches.
A deadly opioid.
On my passenger seat was everything that had destroyed my family, my life, my kids, my world.
My best friend met me in front of where our first meeting would be today.
She knew everything that was going on. Everything.
She was my saving grace too. I already called her on my way. I couldn't believe that the very doctor that told me he would treat him like a kindergartner from here on in, prescribed him Fentanyl once again.
I was just in awe. She didn't know what to say either.
A part of me just had to let go. I knew he was going into rehab soon. There was nothing I could do for him anymore.
Nothing, except be a great mother to our kids.
I text him. I told him I saw the Fentanyl and I took it.
He told me he went to see his doctor. He couldn't deny it. I saw it.
"You had an appointment?"
"No, he was busy so he saw me quickly on the side."
"He saw you on the side! He prescribed you Fentanyl on the side!"
Was I hearing him right? He prescribed an addict a deadly opioid for no medical reason. No X-rays were done. None.

I called him every name in the book for going to see him after all we had been through.
I called him everything except a loser. I had never called him that. But he knew how disgusted I was with him.
I told him I had his keys to the rental and I was not giving them back. Ever.
I told him once again that he was no longer allowed to drive.
I didn't get what he didn't get. He was on Fentanyl once again. And once again he was behind the wheel even after a horrific car accident one week prior.
Nothing phased an addict. They think they are immortal.
I guess in his mind he validated it because he had a script from his asshole doctor.
He didn't even have an appointment. He didn't even know if he had an injury.
He gave him a script on the side. On the side. It made me so sick to my stomach.
I was just going through the motions at this point. Numb.
I made it through the day. As I drove home I was relieved. I knew that once I got home that he would make an appointment to get admitted to rehab. This was it.
"Here's the number."
He answered a lot of questions. And then I heard the best words of my life:
"Okay I'll be there Monday morning, March 16th."
We had an appointment at 10:00 a.m to start the ball rolling for in patient rehab.
I was so happy. Happy for our kids mostly. There was a chance that they'd get their father back.
His phone rang.
"My brother wants us to go upstate for the weekend."
"It's not a good idea. You have to get prepared and ready for rehab Monday."
"Please, come on, let's go. This is my last weekend to spend with the kids before I get admitted. It'll be fun."
He was so down on himself. He knew that his life was out of control. He knew that he had hit rock bottom.

He knew. He knew.

"Ok, I think you're right. One last time. It will be good for all of us."

"We'll take the kids tubing and tobogganing. They will love it."

"Okay. They definitely will."

I was actually excited. I wanted to spend a weekend together as a family.

It would be good for all of us. We hadn't been away together as a family since we moved.

Saturday morning came. We packed the car. I threw his cane in the trunk.

I wanted no part of it. Kids were all buckled in. We were all set to go.

I sat in the driver's seat.

He sat in the passenger seat,

Off we went

to a weekend full of family fun.

Off we went to

a weekend that would change our lives forever.

Sunday Morning (Darkness -34)
Anecdote 34

The kids played in the yard.
It was March14th and there was still a lot of snow on the ground.
They had a great day with their cousins.
He watched and observed. Never did he join them.
He watched from afar.
That ghastly grey was still eminent on his face though.
He didn't look very good. He looked sick.
He was somewhat swollen in the face and in the stomach area.
I couldn't wait until Monday. Rehab would bring him back to healthy. Rehab would bring him back to life.
He was obsessed with finding the boys snow pants. We were all going tubing tomorrow.He couldn't wait to watch them on those snowy hills. The kids were just as excited. We headed out to the local store to search for snow pants. Up and down the aisles. We finally found them. Snowy hills were awaiting us.
But he just wasn't the same. I'm telling you. He just wasn't the same. It was as if he had left his body and someone else took over his soul. Someone else was in that body that day.
We all went out for a nice dinner that night. He seemed at peace. His family knew that he was headed for rehab Monday. We were very sensitive to him and tried to give him words of inspiration.
He was grateful that he had support. When we got home from dinner, the kids went into the other room to play and the adults sat around the table. We were trying to convince him that he needed this help and that rehab would be a new start for him.
He didn't argue at all. He was feeling very down as it was. He felt terrible for all he has caused. He definitely wanted to start over. He definitely needed to start over.

His brother's wife took out her phone.
She wanted him to listen to something.
I had no idea what it was.
Evidently, I accidentally called her the night of the car accident. She never picked up.
She had mine and his brother's conversation recorded as a voicemail. I had no idea I had called.
She prefaced hearing the voicemail by telling him he had to get help.
"Listen to this voicemail. You have to hear the fear in your wife's voice when she saw your car."
He was in shock.
"You have to hear your brother praying that you were okay."
We listened to the voicemail.
It was insane. It was surreal. It was heart wrenching.
You could hear us screaming. You could hear us praying. You could hear the pain
and fear in our voices.
The voicemail captured the very moment that we pulled up to the scene. We were all so shaken by this.
And he was seriously shaken by this the most.
"I need to go for a ride."
For the first time ever, his addiction became so real.
So apparent.
He finally realized first hand that he hurt us. All of us.
He needed to go for a ride. I wouldn't let him go. His brother decided to take him.
His brother adored him and he adored his brother. He wanted the very best for him.
He really did.
We stayed up with the kids and chatted. They loved that they got to stay up late.
We waited up for them.
They came home around 12:30. We all said our good nights and off to bed we went.

I slept with Luca in one bed. And Max slept with his dad in the other bed. He complained that his stomach hurt that night. We weren't sure if it was what he ate or that he just wasn't feeling well.

Morning came. The kids woke up with me. They couldn't wait to go snow tubing.

That morning though, their dad was snoring loudly. So loud that I had to record it. He was definitely one that snored, but we never heard him snore this loud.

We laughed and went into the kitchen to start breakfast. We thought we'd let him sleep a little while longer.

We started breakfast. We promised the kids pancakes. I could see our bedroom from my view in the kitchen. I could see his feet dangling off the bed.

"Go in, but give him a couple more minutes to sleep."

The kids went in. They touched his feet.

His feet didn't move.

Strange.

I saw that the kids tried to wake him again. And again. And again. They were relentless. I saw that his feet still did not move. Not once. I dropped the pan and ran into the bedroom.

"Everybody out. Everybody get out now."

I threw the kids out within seconds. I ran over to him and looked at his face.

My whole life flashed before me.
My whole life with this man flashed before me.
I remembered our children being born.
I remembered how good he was with them.
I remembered the restaurant.
and how he had made it to the top.
The good times.The happy times.
The times that he was a great father to his children.
The times he'd scoop them up when they were hurt.
The times he bought them the best and biggest toy
from the toy store when they were sick.
He was a good father. He loved his boys.
It all flashed before me, right before my very eyes, as I
ran to his bedside.
He was laying on his side as his long rosary bead and
his gold cross laid across his chest.
My screams were like no other.
"Mario!"
"Mario!"

Hail Mary Full of Grace (Darkness-35)

Anecdote 35

The kids were huddled in a corner.
His brother came running in.
There were no needs for words.
We both knew. We both knew.
He was overdosing.
I couldn't believe it. I always knew this could happen, but I never thought it would.
No-one could ever prepare themselves for this. No-one.
His lips had already turned blue. He had vomited all over his pillowcase.
My heart. My heart broke.
Was this it?
We lifted his shirt.
His brother ripped the Fentanyl patch off of his chest.
"Get him on the floor."
We got him on the floor and we took turns giving CPR.
We were frantic. We were in a state of shock. We were trying to save his life.
Neither of us really knew CPR. We only went by what we saw from the movies or from what we learned in health class. We tried our best. Never did I ever think I needed to know CPR. Never did I ever think I needed to know CPR to save my husband's life.
And there were my children huddled in the corner with their cousins watching their mother give CPR to their father.
And there were my children witnessing the unthinkable with their beautiful brown eyes.
Those beautiful brown eyes that I had tried to protect for all these years.
And now I couldn't protect them. I couldn't shield their eyes for the first time in their lives.
I always promised myself that I would be there for them. I always promised myself that I would always protect them from harm.

And here were my children, unprotected.
They had an panoramic view of their father dying.
They witnessed their father, their father, dying in their mother's arms.
Things like this happened in movies. Things like this don't happen in real life.
They just don't.
"Come on Mario. Come on Mario."
"We love you. Don't give up."
Through every breath we instilled in him.
"Please, please hear us. Please. Don't leave us."
My sister in law had called 911.
She began praying.
"Hail Mary full of grace the Lord is with thee."
We continued CPR. We continued praying until the paramedics got there.
It felt like a lifetime. Every breath felt like a lifetime. Every breath felt like my heart was ripping out of my chest, vein by vein.
And during every breath our children looked on.
Scared. Unprotected. Confused. Innocent.
Innocent they were. My babies. Purely innocent.
"Breathe. Breathe."
His rosary bead dangled across his chest accompanied by his gold chain.
Through each of our breaths, it protected his chest.
He hadn't taken it off since the car accident.
Then his brother ripped something off of his foot.
A second Fentanyl patch. He had placed another Fentanyl patch oh his foot.
Holy shit.When?
One Fentanyl patch lasted three days. One Fentanyl patch was 50 to 100 times more potent than morphine. He had two attached to his now motionless body.
Two! Why? Oh my god why? What was he thinking?
And this is why you don't give opioids to an addict. This is why. This is exactly f****ing why.

"Blessed art though amongst women, and blessed is the fruit of thy womb, Jesus.
Holy Mary, Mother of God….."
The Paramedics finally came. They threw us out of the room. The police officer asked us a few questions as the paramedics worked on him. We told her about the Fentanyl. They administered Naloxone, but it may have been too late.
At that point, all his organs had shut down and his heartbeat was only working at ten percent.
He heard us though. He heard us trying to save him. And that for a split second made me happy. He heard us tell him we loved him. He heard us tell him we're not giving up on him. In his last minutes, in his last breaths, he heard us.
I gave my children a huge hug, tears rolled down my face, and for the first time I couldn't console them and tell them that their father would be okay.
I had to leave them there. I had to leave my babies there with their cousins.
Scared, lost, confused.
I went with the police officer as we followed the ambulance. I was numb. She tried making conversation. All I could think about was him. All I could think about were my kids. I was following an ambulance to the hospital that carried the father of my children.
And I know he died.
It was so hard to fathom.
He made so many promises.
He promised our children he would take them to Disneyland next year.
He promised them a good life.
He promised he'd go to rehab.
He promised he'd get better.
He promised he wouldn't die.
He promised.
He promised.

Last Goodbyes (Darkness-36)
Anecdote 36

I was a mess. I was in pure shock.
This part of my memory was somewhat of a blur.
His brother took a separate car up to the hospital. I drove with the officer.
The hospital was around fifteen minutes away. We were upstate. I had no idea where we were nor did I care.
He wanted to make sure that we could get back home.
I couldn't believe that we would be coming home without him.
It was around 9:55 when we pulled in. We were right behind the ambulance.
They wheeled him in. We had to wait outside.
The room was so white and so cold.
This was the worst few minutes of my life. I was shaking.
The doctor came out within minutes to speak to us.
"I'm so sorry. He didn't make it. He has passed away."
I knew. We knew. But to hear it.
To hear it was a whole different story.
We both cried. We both cried out loud.
I cried for my kids the most.
I don't remember saying too much.
"I need you to identify his body."
Oh My God. Please give this job to someone else. I can't do this. I'm not ready.
He took the white sheet off of his face. I lost it.
"Yes, that's him." I couldn't believe I was identifying the body of what was my husband.
The doctor pronounced him dead at 10:20. a.m March 15th, 2009.
"If you'd like, Ill leave you both alone so you can say your last goodbyes."
What? Our last goodbyes. Things like this don't happen to me. Last goodbyes? No, not me. Please not me. Please not me.

We went in.

I hovered over my husband's lifeless body.

It was pure hysteria. There I was lying over my late husband's body to say my goodbyes.

What do you say? What can you possibly say? I wasn't prepared. You are never prepared for this.

His brother waited his turn.

I cried unceasingly during my goodbyes.

"I did everything I could to help you. I was a great wife. I never turned my back on you. But God took you from us. I guess he had bigger plans for you, for us too. I promise to be the best mother I can be to our babies. You were fighting a demon. A demon that was much bigger than you. I promise to take our babies to Disneyland just like you promised. Thank you for so much for giving me such beautiful children. Maybe you'll open up a restaurant again in heaven just like you wanted to do here. Please, please watch over our babies. Rest in Peace."

I started to hyperventilate. I couldn't breathe. I touched his heart with my hand.

I turned my head as his brother said his last goodbyes. It was too hard.

I only caught a bit of his goodbyes.

"I will always take care of your kids, like they are my own. I will always be there for them my brother......"

I couldn't even focus.

I went over to him and I took the rosary beads and his gold cross off of his neck.

My tears dripped onto his chest.

I couldn't be in the hospital anymore. I had to tell my boys their father died. I had to leave.

I had to see my babies. I couldn't wait any longer. It was killing me. I had to tell them.

The officer took me home. I made several phone calls on the way. I do not remember what I said or exactly who I called.

That was a complete blur.

We pulled in and there were my babies waiting for me on the couch.

I grabbed the two of them. I hugged them tightly. I told them I had to talk to them.

They looked up at me with those big brown eyes.

I wished, I wished I could have told him that daddy was fine.

"The angels took your daddy today. He had to go to heaven."

My boys just looked at me in despair and confusion. Luca was almost turning 8 and Max was almost turning 7. What did they even know about heaven? What did they even know about death?

I was so sick to my stomach.

"You see, God needed a hero in heaven and he sent the angels to take him there. Daddy won't be coming home. They needed him….."

I could barely go on. I could barely get the words out.

"I promise the both of you that we will be okay and I promise that we will go to Disneyland just like daddy promised."

I hugged them so tight. I didn't let go.

It was so hard to be so strong when my heart broke for them.

I cried. They cried. We cried together. Our family of four was no longer.

I went outside just to catch my breathe. This was one of the hardest moments of my life.

I wanted to be strong for my kids. I wanted them to know I was okay even though I was dying inside.

My phone rang. I picked up.

"Hello, is this Mrs. Marra?"

"Yes."

"This is the New York Organ Donation agency."

I am speechless. Is this for real? I never thought they'd call. I'm not ready. I still hadn't caught my breath.

'Did you know that your husband was an organ donor?"

"No."

She went on to tell me all the procedures they
would perform. She went into intricate detail.
*"I just told my children that their father died. I can't talk to
you about this. I just can't. Please call my sister. She will
talk on my behalf. You have to respect his wishes,
but whatever you do please save his eyes."*
I don't know why I asked her for this.
It turned out that they were unable to recover any organs.
They had all shut down.
It was just all so overwhelming.
My cousins pulled up to pick us up.
My family was my backbone.
Just the kids and me.
Just the kids and me.
From this point on,
I made a promise to myself.
I made a promise that I would not fall.
That I would not break.
I promised I would show my children a beautiful life
from here on in.
The life that they deserved.
The life that we had signed up for.
No more hurt, no more pain,
and no more crying.
I'm picking up the god damn pieces.
From here on in, I'll never look back.
It's cupcakes and rainbows from here on in.

Made in the USA
San Bernardino, CA
18 August 2018